D0395189

Guerrilla Marketing
FOR THE HOME-BASED
BUSINESS

Guerrilla Marketing
FOR THE HOME-BASED
BUSINESS

Jay Conrad Levinson and Seth Godin

Houghton Mifflin Company
Boston   New York   1995

For information about permission to reproduce selections
from this book, write to Permissions, Houghton Mifflin Company,
215 Park Avenue South, New York, New York 10003.

For information about this and other Houghton Mifflin trade and reference
books and multimedia products, visit The Bookstore at Houghton Mifflin on
the World Wide Web at http://www.hmco.com/trade/

CIP data is available.

ISBN 0-395-74283-8

Printed in the United States of America
DOH   10 9 8 7 6 5 4 3 2 1

ACKNOWLEDGMENTS

Thanks to Steve Lewers and Suzanne Herel at Houghton Mifflin for the help and support that made this book a reality. And to Michael Larsen, Jay's talented agent.

Julie Maner was a key member of the team that created this book. She managed the entire project, from inception to completion. Thanks, Julie.

Thanks also to Mark Henricks, who worked hard to convert our first outlines and drafts into a workable manuscript. We were lucky enough to be assigned one of Houghton's finest copy editors, Luise Erdmann.

Bernadette Grey is the Editor in Chief of Home Office Computing, and a great friend. She had the vision to understand the power of the home office / small office movement years ago, and her work at the magazine, along with the advice and support she's given us, has been instrumental at meshing the power of guerrilla marketing with the effectiveness of the home office.

Fans of Jay and Seth know that they practice what they preach. Jay still works at home, and Seth did for more than seven years. So thanks go to every neighbor, relative, housekeeper and zoning official who made that possible!

This book is dedicated to any spouse, employee, partner, banker or child who has supported someone brave enough to strike out on her own and start a home-based business. Thanks.

CONTENTS

INTRODUCTION
GUERRILLA MARKETING FOR THE HOME-BASED BUSINESS

YOU'RE MAKING HISTORY. YOU'RE PART OF THE FASTEST-growing segment of the American working world, a revolution that is changing the way people work — possibly the largest sociological shift in generations. You work from home.

People who work from home have a job with two bonuses: they don't pay extra rent and they don't commute. No wonder that over the last five years, more than 12 million people have decided to work at home part or full time.

Working from home offers challenges and responsibilities that are very different from those at an office job. No longer a cog in a giant machine, you're a jack of all trades, required to perform tasks from buying paper clips to negotiating big deals. And, of course, you can't blame anything on your boss.

For many home-based workers, the biggest change is the need to represent themselves. Salespeople who have no trouble representing BigCo, Inc., to the world suddenly become humble when forced to talk about themselves. Marketers who can write killer copy for almost any business face writer's block when they need a brochure for their own consulting firm.

The hesitancy to self-promote, to focus on marketing and sales, and to build a network of referrals is one of the biggest problems facing people working at home. Before you get too far into this book, then, you have to make a fundamental decision:

Are you working from home or running a home-based business?

The difference isn't immediately obvious, but it's crucial. In fact, it affects almost all the choices you make.

Dealing with computers, zoning, interruptions, technology, and myriad other hassles can make working from home a problem, but there are countless books that can help you set up an effective arrangement. This book can help you with an entirely different problem. It focuses on building your business.

Marketing is often mentioned by entrepreneurs as the most daunting part of starting a home-based business. People are confident that they can transfer their job skills to the home. They know they can make a first-rate product or deliver a quality service. They don't need help running the copier or paying their bills on time. The question they ask the most often is, "How do I find new business?"

A home-based business is, first and foremost, a business. And like most businesses, the critical elements are figuring out what product or service to provide and then finding customers who need it. Guerrillas running a home-based business focus on increasing their customer base, finding a way to offer more products to more people. This allows them to pick the products and customers that are the most profitable instead of relying on whatever job walks in the door.

The single most important marketing tool for most businesses is word of mouth. The proponents of classical marketing theory spend too little time on this critical element; they worry about annual budgets, nationwide advertising campaigns, and effective coupon distribution.

Guerrilla marketing, on the other hand, is custom-made for the home-based business. When Jay Levinson wrote the first guerrilla marketing book more than a decade ago, working from home was something of a novelty, the sort of thing your mother-in-law would complain about and the neighbors would puzzle over. Yet the lessons outlined in every guerrilla book since then remain relevant to anyone running a business at home.

You might ask: How can I compete with the big guys? How can I possibly hope to grab business away from a company that spends $14 million a year in direct mail alone? How can I build credibility when I'm working out of my house?

In fact, guerrilla marketing gives you the crucial advantage. You can turn the size of your competitors against them, using your flexibility, personal touch, and high-quality products to establish the one-to-one relationships with your customers that they simply cannot match.

You don't need a huge advertising budget because you don't need a huge amount of business. Guerrilla marketing techniques help you focus on the accounts that will make you profitable. It will allow you to make crucial contacts and sell to them in a way that no big business could even consider. And it will give you control over the way you run your business.

Guerrilla marketing techniques are being used by thousands of businesses, large and small. Nike uses billboards to cut through the clutter. NBC uses electronic marketing to make an impact online. And the Fleetwood Corner Café has a frequent buyer club to keep people coming back.

Unfortunately, not every guerrilla marketing weapon is appropriate for the home-based business. It's unlikely that you will buy remnant ad space in *Time* magazine or mount a nationwide coupon campaign that relies on piggybacking. Of the dozens of guerrilla marketing weapons, eleven give home-based businesses a particularly good advantage over the big guys. They will help you develop and implement a strategy that breaks through the clutter and moves the battle for your prospect's business onto a totally different playing field.

- Positioning. Who exactly are you and what do you stand for? While established companies may have a hard time changing their position in the marketplace, adroit guerrillas can assess the competition and totally reposition themselves in a way that sets them apart.

- Customer service. Overwhelming your customers with personal, unexpected service is the single best way to keep them for life. IBM, State Farm, and Wal-Mart have no chance against a motivated entrepreneur who's dedicated to delivering exactly what the customer wants.

- Word of mouth. The guerrilla's best friends are enthusiastic customers who go out of their way to refer people to your business. With a well-conceived guerrilla marketing plan, you can create a large and growing following of this type.

- Publicity. If it's in the newspaper, it must be true. Home-based businesses can use niche media — local papers, trade journals, and newsletters — to establish themselves in their field. Publicity isn't free, but if properly planned, your investment of time and money can return tremendous dividends.

- Printed materials. An effective image in print is critical for most home-based businesses. First impressions generated by flyers, business cards, or brochures are extremely important.

- Direct mail. Mass audience marketers have turned this potentially powerful tool into an intrusion that's wasteful and inefficient. You can turn direct mail on its ear, using it as a way to build personal relationships.

- Newsletters. What if you could create a direct communications pipeline between you and your customers, a marketing piece that prospects would look forward to receiving? A newsletter is a great way to build relationships and turn them into profits.

- Classified ads. Imagine an advertising medium where people come looking to buy from you. Classifieds are useless to most big businesses but can be a solid gold weapon for the home-based business.

- Networking. Virtually every buying decision is based on trust. And trust is generated through personal relationships. By building an ever-growing base of positive referrals, you can leave your competition in the dust.

- The telephone. The great marketing equalizer is the telephone. By definition, a telephone conversation is a one-to-one interaction — which is perfect for you. You offer the prospect a chance to talk directly with the CEO. Your competition can't do that.

- Closing the sale. All the marketing in the world won't help you if you can't turn interested prospects into paying customers. Entrepreneurs often have trouble with this critical step, but we'll show you some easy ways to make it work.

HOW TO USE THIS BOOK

The most important lesson a home-based businessperson can gain from this book is how to think like a guerrilla. Learning how to use your size and speed to your advantage is a critical lesson. You have countless opportunities to create profitable niches in businesses that everyone else believes are saturated.

You'll need to learn that you're now vice president of marketing. Business won't appear on your doorstep. It will come as the result of a consistent, long-term campaign to establish relationships and turn them into sales.

The single biggest mistake home-based business owners make is that they give up too soon. It might take six months, eighteen months, or two years before a prospect is finally ready to say yes. Instead of switching from one get-rich scheme to another, pick your niche and focus. And hang in there.

The second biggest mistake? Not having a plan. To embark on a program using many tools and tactics without a plan is foolish. Instead, write down how you expect to proceed, how much time and money you intend to invest, and post it on the wall. This road map will make it easier for you to stay the course.

Read these eleven chapters to decide which specific tactics will work for your business. Outline exactly which tools you'll be using and when.

Marketing is not something you can do all at once. It's an ongoing process, a habit that will result in significant returns.

Marketing is not free. The tactics described in this book will cost you time and money. But marketing isn't an expense, it's an investment. Businesses that make regular, healthy contributions of time and money to their marketing budgets thrive. Those that skimp, that cut back in the slow times, wither. Like any other investment, marketing delivers the best results if you contribute funds regularly and think like a guerrilla.

WORKING FROM HOME

Jay Levinson has been running a profitable business from his home in California for more than fifteen years. He's applied the lessons outlined in this book to create a worldwide business. Guerrilla Marketing International is so successful that Jay is able to support his family and only work three days a week.

Seth Godin started his company in his house in 1986. For eight years Seth Godin Productions expanded, at one point using six rooms, the garage, and the kitchen. With the birth of Seth's son, Alexander, it was pretty clear that someone had to move out. Fortunately, Seth found a nice office for his dozen employees, and Alex didn't have to sleep in the street.

POSITIONING
CARVING A NICHE IN THE MARKETPLACE

HERE'S A QUICK POSITIONING QUIZ. Match the celebrity to the sport:

Jackie Gleason	Skiing
Cindy Crawford	Golf
Gerald Ford	Bowling

Which celebrity goes with which sport? If you're like most people, you'll quickly envision Cindy Crawford as the ski bunny, Gerald Ford as the golfer, and Jackie Gleason, who played the blue-collar, beer-drinking Ralph Kramden on TV, as the bowler. In fact, Gleason actually spent a lot of time on the slopes and playing golf as well.

The reason we make quick categorizations is that there are too many magazines, advertisements, newscasts, celebrities, businesses, brands, and sports to keep track of. Faced with this deluge of information, our brains respond by pigeonholing people into categories.

Like it or not, your business will be pigeonholed, too. You may be pigeonholed as unreliable, expensive, or, if you take control of the situation, the best home business in your field. It's up to you. That's why this is the single most important chapter in this book.

As a home-based businessperson, you need to use pigeonholing to your advantage by creating your very own position within your industry of choice. Then your position is the segment of the market that you choose based on your strength and the competition's weakness. It's where you fit.

Marty Winston, a home-based public relations consultant, took control of the way people think of his business. He refused to be thought of as just another public relations flack working out of his basement.

Instead, he's billed himself as "the most e-mail knowledgeable PR agent in the universe."

Think that sounds crazy? Pointless? Impossible to back up? You're wrong on all three counts.

With his weekly electronic newsletter, extensive database of journalists' e-mail addresses, and good understanding of how to use electronic messaging in marketing and PR, this home-based guerrilla backs up his claim absolutely. Familiar with Marty's business, any client who believes in (or can be convinced of) e-mail's marketing value will go to him first.

Of course, Marty isn't going to sign up every prospective client. But that's okay, because he gets the lion's share of business from people who believe in his position as the world's best e-mail PR person.

7Up is the Uncola, for people who don't like Pepsi or Coke. Apple is "computers for the rest of us." And Avis promises to try harder because it's No. 2. For a while, Tylenol was in danger of being positioned as the pain reliever that could kill people. Only astute marketing rescued it from this horrible fate.

You may not know it, but your business has a position in the marketplace, too. Every business does, home-based or multinational.

WHY POSITIONING?

There are two unassailable facts that force every guerrilla to adopt a position before someone does it for him:

1. The marketplace is cluttered with competition.

2. For your home-based business to succeed, you need to cut through that clutter.

The cluttered marketplace is a fact. An overwhelming number of products, services, and messages reach the consumer every day. Last year, 17,000 new products (or 57% of the total number of products in supermarkets) were introduced in supermarkets. In one decade, from the early 1980s to the early 1990s, the estimated dollar volume of advertising in the United States almost doubled. Corporations now pour more than $100 billion a year into getting their message out. That means $400 worth of advertising is directed at each man, woman, and child in the country in the form of tens of thousands of advertisements and billboards.

Clearly, as a home-based business you have to cut through this clutter. You must set yourself apart, and you can't do it by outspending Procter & Gamble. And you can't do it by hoping that consumers will make the effort to discover you.

Many people persist in believing that their business will be treated differently by the jaded market. They care far more about their business than anyone else, and they believe that consumers will make the effort to discover them.

Don't make the mistake of assuming that your potential customers know or care about your business as much as you do.

Here's an example of what we're talking about: A major company, best known for its educational software, wanted to remind consumers of its entertainment line. After hours and hours of meetings, they finally decided to painstakingly color-code their product boxes. A gold strip on the box meant it contained educational software, a blue strip meant entertainment, and a blue and gold strip meant both.

The result was that the the consumer didn't notice. At all. The company held the position for educational software, and all the color-coded strips in the world weren't going to change that.

Here are a few well-known pigeons and their pigeonholes:

Nike — shoes for athletes.

Keds — sneakers for kids.

Timberland — boots for hikers.

Of course, Nike makes boots, Keds makes shoes for grown-ups, and Timberland makes shirts. Doesn't matter. Each one has established a position in the mind of the consumer.

You can resist this process and try not to be positioned, but chances are you're going to be positioned anyway, probably in the vast, unproductive pile called Other. That's exactly where you don't want to end up.

Roslyn Goldman is a home-based art appraiser and consultant — a fairly amorphous profession. Rather than trying to be all things to all people, she has hammered out a specific niche. All of her sales and marketing materials have her positioning statement emblazoned on the front: "Appraiser of fine art." She also included the following statement on her brochure: "Complete art services for private, professional and corporate collectors, galleries, schools and universities, insurance and moving companies, and lawyers for estate purposes."

THE ART OF POSITIONING

You've got a head start. As a guerrilla, you understand the power of positioning. Now you've got to take advantage of that knowledge.

Be First.

If you're the first in a category, you can usually invent your own position. In marketing (as in stock car racing, child rearing, and nuclear physics), no two bodies can occupy the same space at the same time. If you get to a position first, you have to be removed before someone else can take it over. Here are some examples:

- Miller Lite. The first beer that tasted great but was less filling. It took blunders on Miller's part and millions and millions of dollars spent by competitors to unseat it.

- Sears. It started the first chain of department stores after World War II and dominated retailing for forty years.

- Federal Express. There are cheaper, faster, easier ways to send a package. Yet FedEx still dominates, because it owns the position.

- Roller Blades. So strong in its position that the brand name is almost generic for the entire category.

  Warning! There are two caveats:

1. Just because you're first in a position doesn't mean you get to stay there forever. Sears failed to respond to Wal-Mart's challenge and gave up its position as retailer to the middle class. The fabled catalog for small-town and rural Americans was replaced by Wal-Mart's stores.

2. It doesn't matter who is technically first in the marketplace with a product or service. The first to get a product or service into the consumer's mind owns the position. Think of it: there was overnight delivery before FedEx, and recordings of Gregorian monks were commonplace before the *Chant* CD came out, but these marketers were the first to stake a claim in the consumer's consciousness.

  You don't have to be a member of the Fortune 500 to be first. Home-based guerrillas can be the first in several ways:

- You can be the first to offer a product or service in your community.

- You can be the first to tailor a general-use item for a specific audience.

- You can be the first to market a product at a new price point.

- You can be the first to offer an alternative to an existing product or service.

- You can be the first to tap into a soon-to-be major market that larger companies have overlooked.

Opportunities to combine marketing elements into a proprietary niche are virtually endless, especially for guerrillas, who don't have the entire world as a customer. Remember, Frito-Lay can't afford to introduce a new product that doesn't promise to generate $100 million in sales the first year. That means Frito-Lay discards many, many snack products that would sustain a guerrilla in imperial style.

Barbara Coole-Richman, who started a home-based catalog for children's natural fiber clothing, is a master at finding new niches for her products. Aside from being the first to sell clothes devoid of chemicals and additives, she was also the first to target parents of disabled children. Barbara took the position that she doesn't sell clothing. She sells "hypoallergenic clothing to parents whose children have special needs," and she is very successful at it. Is she worried about Levi's, the Gap, or Wal-Mart? What do you think?

Naturally, few of us have the privilege of inventing a major category. With over 15 million businesses operating in the U.S., your chances of coming up with even a minor category that's really new are slim.

But all is not lost. Even if your market niche is cramped with competitors, you have two powerful positioning choices.

Reposition the Competition or Reinvent a Category.

- 7Up floundered until it announced it was the Uncola. The more Coca-Cola and Pepsi advertised, the more they helped 7Up.

- IBM touted its huge size for years. Then Apple repositioned IBM as big brother, a lumbering monolith that didn't have the little guy in mind.

- Avis did poorly until it conceded that it was No. 2 to Hertz. By focusing on the underdog attitude of their employees, they turned Hertz's size into a negative.

- Johnson & Johnson's Tylenol isn't acetaminophen. It's "non-aspirin pain reliever." It might not sound much different, but the change in

 One way to figure out your niche is to ask your existing clients. If many of them hired you for the same reason, there's your answer.

semantics worked wonders. By proudly pointing out that there's no aspirin in Tylenol, it repositioned the leader.

- Linda Abraham edits and writes résumés and college application essays. She faced too much competition and not enough business. But once she began focusing her efforts on separating herself from the competition, her business took off. Linda realized that her competition wasn't focused on a specific market — they were all generalists. She wrote a pamphlet containing tips on writing graduate school application essays and began giving lectures on writing personal statements, clearly positioning herself as an expert on the subject. Now any student in Los Angeles looking for help with a graduate school application is likely to hear about Linda.

- When Hank Walshak started his home-based marketing and public relations company in Pittsburgh, the first thing he did was position himself away from the competition. While most public relations companies try to impress potential clients with big offices, fancy meals, and leather armchairs, Hank stressed the fact that his company was small, yet attentive, and could respond to clients' needs in a more personal and timely manner. He effectively repositioned the big agencies as bureaucratic, impersonal corporations with slow turnaround times. The more the big PR firms flaunted their large staffs, big office buildings, and extensive client lists, the more they actually helped Hank improve his hold on his niche.

If you don't want to reposition the competition, your other option is to "invent" a new category. You don't have to be Thomas Edison to do this. Brand-new major categories of goods and services are created all the time by subdividing an existing category. Mail-order computers and miniblind cleaning services are good examples of spin-off categories started by home-based guerrillas that grew into sizable industries. Marty Winston subdivided, or wrinkled, the concept of a PR agency to come up with an agency specializing in e-mail-driven public relations campaigns.

There are hundreds of freelance writers and public relations professionals out there, but not many that cater to the construction industry. David Wood is one of them. From his experience working for a contractors' trade organization, he realized that as a group, contractors are not very good at marketing themselves. So, David writes newsletters, brochures, and promotional pieces for contractors, real estate agents, and architects. Because he specializes, he is known as the expert in his field, and when people in the construction industry need marketing help, they look to David first.

Or you can take two concepts and put them together. Once there were educational catalogs and there were catalogs for Hispanic children. But there were no catalogs of educational products for Hispanic children before Theresa Iglesias-Solomon's catalog.

Try this exercise: take a general description of what you do, such as sell insurance, consult, or give seminars. Now add a qualifier that exactly describes your major product or competitive advantage. You've instantly repositioned yourself in a new category. Here are some examples:

- You don't sell insurance, you sell EQUIPMENT INSURANCE TO SMALL BUSINESS OWNERS.

- You don't sell government consulting, you sell consulting for STRIP MINING COMPANIES.

- You don't give motivational speeches, you give speeches that culminate in the entire audience WALKING ON HOT COALS!

Obviously, not every potential customer is a small business owner, a strip mining company, or wants to walk on hot coals (although they may by the time you're through). That's part of the cost of finding a niche: you can't be all things to all people.

You need discipline to narrow your niche, but it pays off. Can you name five successful companies that are all things to all people?

Levi Strauss? It's the world's biggest apparel company, but it doesn't make expensive formal wear.

IBM? It's the world's largest computer company, but it doesn't make fax machines.

General Motors? It makes more motor vehicles than any other automotive company, but not a single motorcycle.

Even a giant like Microsoft, which is several times larger than any of its software competitors, ignores some products, some price points, some niches. The lesson here is that no business, no matter how big, survives without a niche of its own.

HOW TO POSITION YOURSELF

You may be thinking: "Wow! If only I could be Jobs and Wozniak putting together the first Apple computer in that garage. Or a business

 Define your niche in thirteen words or less. If you can't, how can you expect your clients to?

school student named Fred Smith with an idea for overnight delivery and a company called Federal Express. Then I'd have position! But I'm just me. I don't really have much of a position. So I'll have to muddle along without one."

Hold everything. You may not be about to found a great corporation (then again, who knows?), but your home-based business can't stay afloat without conscious positioning. Arriving at such a position is *not* a matter of luck, it's part art and part science, but there are discernible steps to reaching this goal:

1. Do Your Research.

Ask yourself these crucial questions:
What is my position now?

A customer, employee, competitor, or knowledgeable objective observer (preferably all four) can provide valuable input.
What position do my competitors occupy?

When Donald Trump set out to be a celebrity, he may have done an analysis of all the other celebrities: starlets, movie hunks, villains, politicos, etc. But no one was filling the millionaire mogul playboy niche. Here was an opportunity!
What position would I like to occupy?

Be realistic. It's unlikely you're going to become the largest PR firm in your industry or the nation's highest-paid copywriter. Guerrillas can prosper greatly while being the second or third or thirty-third provider of a service, as long as something distinguishes their offering.
Who are the competitors in my desired position?

Sometimes there is no position available in a crowded or depressed market. We'd argue that starting a large overnight delivery company, for instance, probably isn't that prudent.

But the markets without *any* new positions are few and far between. Remember, marketers make the mistake of going up against market leaders on their own turf. The best product and best execution won't help if a market leader is selling the same benefit in the same way for half the price.
Is the niche big enough?

There's a gaping niche in supplying breathing apparatus to residents of the far side of the moon. But you'd be the only supplier to a small, in fact nonexistent, market. Your niche has to be narrow but deep enough to support your business.

As a home-based guerrilla, you have lower overhead than most businesses. You can go after markets that are so small or offer such thin margins that others could never even consider them. This is a key advantage. But even you have your limits. If the sales aren't there, you shouldn't be, either.

What is it going to take to tap into my target market?

It costs money to "own" a niche, and some are more expensive than others.

Do I have what it takes to stake out this position?

Just because a niche exists, would support a business, and is exploitable doesn't mean you are up for the task. For example, providing overnight delivery of organ transplant supplies may be a profitable niche, but if you're not willing to work at it with 100%

> Tom's of Maine is one of the greatest home-based success stories. Tom and Kate Chappell started their business at their kitchen table with a $5,000 loan from a friend. Competition in the toothpaste market had defeated many larger businesses with much bigger budgets. Instead of fighting a losing battle, the Chappells repositioned themselves and their product. They don't sell toothpaste. They sell sugar-free, all natural, environmentally friendly toothpaste. When they started, they had essentially no competition in their niche. Tom's has grown by 25% to 30% every year since 1970.

quality, 24 hours a day, people are going to die. That may not be a risk you're willing to take on a corporate or personal level.

Here is an example of how good research can pay off:

After Theresa Iglesias-Solomon came up with her idea for a mail order catalog business, she spent over a year doing exhaustive market research to answer a tailored set of questions. She asked:

1. Is there a Hispanic market for catalog items?

2. What kinds of products should I sell?

3. What does the Hispanic consumer market look like demographically and psychographically?

4. Who should develop my catalog?

The most important decision that Theresa made was her answer to question 2. She knew from the start that marketing products to the Hispanic population was a good idea, but it wasn't focused enough. So she studied her market and made the tough decisions that were necessary to define her particular niche. As a result, her Niños catalog offers educational products for Hispanic children and is both unique and in demand.

Sandra Beckwith is the home-based publisher of "The Do(o) Little Report," a newsletter for women that takes a lighthearted look at male behavior. She checked newsletter directories, held focus groups, and talked to newsletter industry experts to determine if there was a place for her newsletter. So before she ever published the first issue, she knew nobody else was putting out a product like hers. Even better, she knew there was a demand for it. She combined the first issue with a huge publicity campaign and generated over 15,000 subscriber inquiries in ten months.

2. Make a Positioning Map.

The easiest way to find a niche is to draw a map of your market and see where your competitors fit. For example, consider the market for toothpaste:

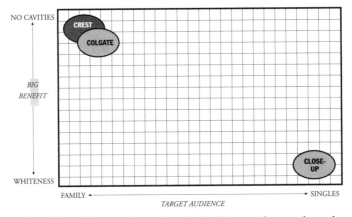

When Close-Up was introduced, the big toothpaste brands were all fighting for one position. They wanted to be "the family toothpaste that fights cavities." Close-Up was brilliantly positioned as a toothpaste for single young adults who care about whiter teeth, fresh breath, and sex appeal a lot more than cavities.

Obviously, the choice of the axes of this graph is crucial. Knowing which ones to choose requires the insight that separates a successful guerrilla from a failed marketer.

When Tom's of Maine decided to introduce its toothpaste, they drew a different map. Instead of using cavities and sex appeal as axes, they used health food stores and natural ingredients.

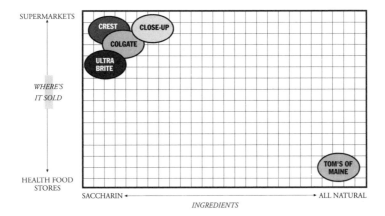

Tom's of Maine chose to reposition on the basis of where the product was sold and what it contained. By redefining toothpaste's position in the marketplace, they established a successful niche for healthy toothpaste.

The result — it created a whole new market, and for more than five years, Tom's was the only major brand of toothpaste that was all-natural. A person shopping at a health food store had essentially one choice when selecting toothpaste: Tom's of Maine.

To make your own positioning map, you need to:

1. List the businesses competing for your consumer. Include everybody. If you sell beef jerky, count the makers of pretzels, chips, carrot sticks, and other snack foods.

2. Outline each brand's product position. How is it different from the rest? One may be cheapest. Another is priciest. A third is for people who prefer imports. Your competitors' positions will delineate your own.

3. Plot each relevant product or brand on the grid below. Put one variable such as price, quality, or service on the bottom axis. The other axis measures a second variable and should be something complementary, like distribution or image.

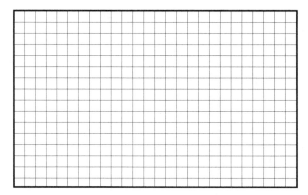

4. Now think of another variable, one that plays to your strengths and everyone else's weaknesses. Plot a new graph and find your niche in it.

In virtually every market, there is an opportunity to reposition the competition and create your own niche. Use this positioning process to discover who your competition is and how you can outposition them.

Positioning is a dynamic game. Every move you make has an effect on your competition and the market. Reposition the competition by coming up with a new product feature that nobody else has. Better yet, find something that the competition has, and appeal to the consumers who don't like that feature! Here are some examples of ways to reposition your company and your product:

- Many people don't like computers for precisely the same reasons others love them: they're powerful and flexible. The market for "it's not a computer, it's a dedicated word processor" writing tools may not be huge, but Smith Corona does quite well with it.

- Lots of shoppers wouldn't be caught dead in Wal-Mart. They despise it for the same reason others patronize it: its low-price image. As a result, high-priced specialty stores coexist nicely with the Bentonville behemoth.

- Telephones are powerful conveniences for most people most of the time. But folks occasionally want to get away from the incessant jangle. For them, a resort hotel that advertises "no phones in rooms" is appealing.

 Put your positioning statement on your business card and your letterhead.

This is the brochure that Stevie Ann Rinehart used to launch her home-based illustration service. It helps her establish the unique position of being an illustrator/cartoonist who specializes in helping businesses add humor to their own marketing materials.

ONCE YOU'VE GOT IT, ARTICULATE IT

It's not enough to know your position. You have to be able to communicate it to others.

People get bombarded with so much information today that they won't — and probably can't — absorb complex positioning statements. So live by this rule: if you can't describe your position in two sentences, it's not a position worth expressing.

Think of Marty Winston and his e-mailed publicity newsletter. There are thousands of PR firms out there, but Marty is "the most e-mail knowledgeable PR agent." In fact, most of Marty's customers probably think of him as "the e-mail expert," an even briefer title.

Think about it. When you have to put a label on a file folder, how long is that label? A perfect length for someone to "file away" and remember, right? An ideal positioning statement shouldn't be much longer. Here are some examples:

- Downtown Milwaukee's only vegetarian diner

- The pet store for bird lovers

- The all-natural exterminator

- The rush printer for people on a budget

- The Brazilian travel experts

Once you've come up with a possible positioning statement, run it by people in your industry. Ask:

- Do they understand it? An electrician who advertises "100 Amp And Up Service" to homeowners isn't going to help his position because few people know what that means.

- Have you staked out a new position? Dozens of pizzerias in New York City claim to be the "original" Ray's. That position is so well trodden, nobody pays any attention to the word "original."

- Is your position relevant? The tallest left-handed knife sharpener in Omaha may be unique, but it holds no benefit to the user. Your business must be positioned to emphasize meaningful strengths.

 TIP! The name of your business contributes to your position in the marketplace. Compare "John Gross and Co." with "Accurate Information Research." Pick a name that will have some meaning to your prospects, thereby making your marketing job a little easier.

There are as many consultants in the state of California as there are fault lines. Yet there's only one person who can help your mining company get a permit to do surface mining in the rich soil east of Los Angeles. And that's Ingrid Elsel. The big guys can't focus nearly as tightly from their 32nd-floor offices in downtown L.A. as Ingrid can from her enclosed patio-turned-office in Ventura. In fact, the guys in L.A. never even thought to provide consultation to mining companies until Ingrid came along. By carving out a niche and dominating it, Ingrid has created a lucrative business and has positioned herself as *the* mining expert in California.

MAKE YOUR POSITION CLEAR

Once you've decided how to express your position in words, get the word out. Put it on your advertisements, brochures, business cards, checks, coupons, direct mail business reply cards, direct mail envelopes, direct mail letters, gift certificates, invoices, letterhead, newsletter masthead, promotional gifts, proposals, signs, and thank-you notes.

Do more than just state your position in words. Make sure that all your materials convey the position in visual terms, too. If you specialize in fine stationery, your letterhead had better be pretty ritzy. If your business specializes in tours for teenagers, make sure your ads have a youthful look and feel to them.

You will make your communication job much easier by coming up with a positioning tag that's short. "A Kinder, Gentler Fur Coat" describes Donna Salyers's synthetic fur coat business in memorable terms, yet fits easily on her business card. Theresa Iglesias-Solomon lets everyone know what Niños is by simply looking at her colorful stationery. It says "Bilingual Educational Products."

Stevie Ann Rinehart turned her part-time freelance illustration business into a full-time venture almost a year ago. When approaching prospective clients, she focuses like a laser. She pitches them on producing company literature and promotional pieces that include her cartoons. Everything she sends out — from her letterhead, designed to look like a humorous cartoon, to her direct mail piece, which is full of cartoons — articulates her position. Businesses that want to inject a little humor into their marketing approach know to contact Stevie first. She's the expert.

But it's not enough to find a tantalizing opportunity and come up with a slogan that resonates with a target market. Your business decisions must all reflect your position. If you call yourself "The 3-Hour Printer," every aspect of your business must emphasize speed. Taking on a contract that calls more for painstaking, fine quality than quick turn-around will dilute your emphasis.

That sounds obvious. But it's a good thing to keep in mind, because you may tend to forget it and go chasing off after markets your business isn't positioned to serve — and lose your real position while you're at it. Tiffany could probably sell a lot of cheap costume jewelry for a while. But then its position as a deluxe jeweler would be ruined.

2 CUSTOMER SERVICE
AN INVESTMENT IN WORD OF MOUTH

MIKE LEE RUNS ICONS & IMAGES, A TYPESETTING SERVICE for desktop publishers. For most people, typesetting is typesetting. If Mike decided to compete on price alone, he'd soon be outgunned by bigger competitors.

Instead, Mike tells his customers that they can leave jobs at his shop any time, any way they want. They can use regular mail. They can use FedEx. They can use his friendly computer bulletin board to upload jobs via modem day or night.

And if they don't have time to drop by or mail a job in? If they don't have a computer with a modem? Mike will pick up the job himself, take it back to his office, and, if at all possible, deliver the completed project the same day.

SERVICE COUNTS

In survey after survey, in all kinds of industries, the number one reason that customers give for switching suppliers is not price, convenience, or location. It's poor service. If you believe that you're in a commodity business, you're doomed to lousy margins and an overwhelming marketing challenge. But if you redefine yourself as a service business, you can eliminate the competition by redefining them as mere commodities.

By focusing on service, you'll capture and keep the most profitable customers. Remember, 80% of your business comes from 20% of your customers. Compared to the rest, those 20% are spending a lot of money with you. They can afford to go anywhere they want for what you sell them. Why do they stick with you? Odds are, customer service is a big reason.

Customer service builds customer loyalty like nothing else. Customer service generates repeat buyers. Sales to repeat buyers are much less costly (and therefore more profitable) than sales to new customers. The money you invest in service will pay off in reduced new customer marketing costs — which translates into increased profits.

Customer service is everything from your turnaround time to your product quality, from attention to detail to apologies for mistakes. Use your size to your advantage. You can take the time to wow each and every customer, both existing and potential, with the attention you give them.

YOU CAN BE A LEADER IN CUSTOMER SERVICE

It's easy to get bogged down in the details of customer service. What's important? What should you focus on?

Answer: It's all important. Customers remember your little service failures as well as (and maybe better than) your major successes.

The most important elements of customer service for most businesses are speed, quality, personal service, accessibility, flexibility, and after-sale service. Checking your performance in these areas can help you home in on the most critical service considerations in your business. And if your business is different, you'll understand exactly how it is different.

Speed.

Speed is probably the simplest element of good customer service. Almost any industry can be transformed by the introduction of speed.

No one knew they wanted photos so quickly until one-hour processing came along. Two weeks was considered a reasonable time to wait for new software until MacConnection started shipping software overnight by Airborne Express. Until EPI Graphics started offering same-day color copies, people were willing to wait a week.

You can literally build a business off little more than world-class speed.

 Nurture the human bond as well as a business bond with your customers. Do them favors, educate them, offer gifts, play favorites, take them to the ball game or the opera. Your customers deserve this treatment. If you won't give it to them, somebody else will.

Quality.

Quality has been the mantra of business for more than a decade. Unfortunately, most businesses don't really understand what quality means. We think of it as the answer to the question: Does the product do what the customer expects it to do?

Big companies often leave the door open to high-quality guerrillas because their businesses are built on selling a little to a lot of customers. With millions of car buyers out there, General Motors can afford to manufacture a few lemons. With a few thousand, a few hundred, or even fewer customers, you can't afford so much as one sour grape.

Quality doesn't necessarily mean making the very best product, regardless of price. Standard typesetting quality is 1,200 dots per inch. But there are typesetting machines that can produce almost five times that resolution. If customers need a magnifying glass to see the difference in their printed proofs, does the extra quality justify the extra expense?

Tom Chapman, the home-based owner of Chapman Design Concepts, used customer service to break into the business of refurbishing foreclosed properties for re-sale. Tom saw an opportunity when he realized that most bankers hate the red tape associated with this kind of renovation. He turned that to his advantage and focused on customer service. Whereas a traditional company might take months to redo one house, Tom can do it in two weeks. That's very appealing to a banker, who wants to sell off the property as soon as possible. Tom has sped up the sales process by providing his clients with quotes overnight by fax. His competitors take up to a week. With quick, high-quality service, Tom generated the word of mouth he needed to make his business a huge success...and he's never spent a dime on advertising.

Quality is in the eyes of the customer. Give customers the quality they ask for (or just a little bit more). Do your best to deliver perfect quality. You're never going to get it right every time. If you don't, stand behind your product with a no-hassle guarantee.

Guarantees.

Guarantees often scare home-based business people. If you just do a few dozen major transactions a year, like many home-based guerrillas, more than a couple of big refunds or reworks could mean financial catastrophe. Won't your customers take advantage of you?

The way we see it, there are two possibilities. The first is that your customer is unhappy. If this is true, he or she will tell friends, generating negative word of mouth. That costs you a lot. It's better to give a refund or redo the work and turn an angry customer into a satisfied one.

The second is that your customer is happy. In that case, he or she won't want a refund because your business will be helpful in the future.

There are two exceptions to the guarantee rule:

- Your product or service is expensive and quality is difficult to measure. For example, if you sell ads in a magazine, refunding the purchase price of an ad that doesn't generate responses is dangerous.

- Your product or service is sold to strangers who are unlikely to do business with you ever again. Unfortunately, there *are* people who will rip you off.

In both cases, you should still offer a guarantee (in writing!), but it should set reasonable conditions. If one-time customers are your mainstay, you can hamstring cheaters by providing a make-good instead of a cash refund. If the quality of your product or service is highly subjective, require customers to inspect it extensively and accept it before delivery. That will nip many frivolous guarantee-invokers in the bud.

If you do offer a guarantee, make it a selling tool, a demonstration of the confidence you have in your product. Some big companies use this technique to great advantage. Sears has guaranteed every product it has ever sold. If you use a Craftsman wrench for thirty years and then break it, you'll get a new one — no questions asked. Few people ever take Sears up on the guarantee, but they feel good knowing it's there.

Go to McDonald's. Buy a Big Mac and a milkshake. Eat half the Big Mac and drink half the milkshake. Put the Big Mac in the milkshake and take it up to the counter. Say "I can't drink this milkshake. There's a Big Mac in it." You'll get a full refund. Why? Because even though the occasional wise guy takes advantage, the average customer knows that there will never be a question about quality at McDonald's. And that's worth millions in word of mouth.

Here are the elements of a really useful guarantee:

- Have a meaningful payoff. Ideally, you should reimburse your customer for any loss incurred by using your faulty product or service, not just the amount paid. Prestone's antifreeze guarantee, for instance, says it will replace a car's radiator — not just the $8 bottle of antifreeze the customer bought. You may not be able to pay someone back for every conceivable damage. But your payout should be

 According to a recent study, a satisfied customer tells one friend; a dissatisfied one tells nine friends. A guerrilla interested in positive word of mouth needs to focus on service.

appealing enough for the customer to think "I'm not going to lose anything by trying this product."

- Make it easy to collect. If your guarantee requires a notarized, dated sales receipt and detailed usage log proving your product wasn't abused before it failed, you may as well not have a guarantee at all. Make it easy for your customers to collect while still protecting yourself from fraud.

  And do it fast. A guarantee delayed may as well be a guarantee denied. The time to pay off on a guarantee is before the customer has decided never to do business with you again.

- Cost nothing extra. Don't kid yourself that by selling an extended service warranty you're giving people a guarantee. Consumers are jaded. They know that an extra-cost warranty is just another way for a manufacturer not to guarantee its work.

  Some innovative guerrilla guarantees we've come across are:

- A copywriter who guarantees that his direct mail letter will outpull the existing standard or your money back.

- A carpet cleaning company that will clean one rug in your house. If you don't like it, the cleaners leave, at no charge. If you do, they clean the rest of the house.

- A freelance artist who promises to deliver everything by deadline or there's no charge.

  Marjorie Desgrosselier, a home-based information broker, has no hesitation about naming the time that customer service paid off for her the most. It started with a mistake she made. The client was not pleased. Marjorie could have written the client off as already lost. Instead, she redid the job for free. The client was so pleased with the second effort that he not only became a steady repeat customer, but he also referred other clients to her.

Personal Service.

Personal service above and beyond the call of duty is the guerrillas' hallmark. It's their edge, their reason for being. The guerrilla who doesn't provide personal attention is missing out on a major marketing advantage over any rivals.

Superb service starts well before the sale, when you find out exactly what the customer expects of you personally.

Scott Bruce of Panther Advertising and Marketing routinely spends two full weeks with each prospect. At no charge, he talks to employees, executives, and customers, learning about the business. Only then does he propose a complete marketing and advertising plan to the company. He asks for a monthly retainer based on how much time the company wants him to spend helping it implement his plan over the next year. For example, a copy center asked him to spend an hour a week in the shop to implement a marketing plan.

Since Scott started, he has converted an astounding 100% of his prospects into clients. The two weeks he spends with each prospect before creating a proposal is the secret to his success. It's expensive for him to spend that much time, but clearly it's very effective.

Specialized, one-of-a-kind service can make a guerrilla business stand out even if it has many competitors. A home-based desktop publisher we know stakes her entire business on the level of service she provides for her clients. For example, she designs and typesets a monthly newspaper for one client. The paper's content is timebound and the printing deadlines are tight. More often than not, the desktop publisher receives late or incomplete information from the client.

Most typesetting and design houses would be unable to meet the deadlines, given such demands. Our guerrilla takes the material as it comes and delivers the newspaper on time, every time — and without complaint. Think the client is likely to go anywhere else?

Accessibility.

When a company hires ad agency Ogilvy & Mather, it doesn't get to work directly with master adman David Ogilvy. But your clients get your full attention. That's a key selling point for a home-based business.

People who use Simian Id Software can talk with home-based founder and owner Don Branson about how his file management programs will work on their systems. He wrote the programs and he supports them. Microsoft can't compete at this level.

Customers of Ontario's Computer Aided Services & Training can call guerrilla owner Pattianne Turner in the evenings and on weekends to ask about a menu layout or the typeface for a wedding program.

Business plan writer Marcia Layton emphasizes the personal nature of her business when talking to prospects. Often clients want to know which member of her staff will be handling their plan. Marcia turns the

TIP! Make customer service your competitive edge. It's the one area where you, as a home-based guerrilla, have the greatest advantage over the big guys. Do it better than anyone else and people will notice.

question to her advantage by explaining that as the only employee, she handles each plan herself.

You can also stress your accessibility in the way you allow customers to contact you. Put your home number on your business card along with your e-mail address and fax number. Or get a beeper and pass that number out, too.

Flexibility.

You don't have a policy manual. You have no legal department or precedents to worry about. Instead, you can offer customers the flexibility they want.

A huge company has tightly controlled systems to make it as efficient as possible. But those systems do not allow for special requests. Home-based guerrillas can. They take advantage of their flexibility to attract lifelong customers by satisfying their unusual requests.

Doll designer Donna Hawley got a call from a customer who wanted a blue Santa Claus doll. Ordinarily, Donna sells Santa in red. Santa *is* red — everybody knows that. But Donna made a blue Santa for her customer.

Make your flexibility clear. Print it on your rate sheet or your brochure. Remember "Special orders don't upset us"? For a while, that slogan made Burger King a legitimate threat to McDonald's.

We're not suggesting you give away the store. But don't dismiss a request just because it's extraordinary.

Service after the Sale.

Why offer service after the sale? Because the first sale is nothing but a step on the way to the next sale. And the service you provide leads to repeat customers, the best, most profitable kind of customers to have.

Show active appreciation for your customer's patronage. Free tune-ups, phone calls to check in, onsite service — they're all little ways to show your customers that you care.

Mike Lee at Icons & Images sends a thank-you card along with every job. Not only is it a nice touch, but it provides instructions on how best to handle the product so it doesn't get damaged. Sometimes Mike also includes a little sticker offering the customer a discount on the next job.

When you're a thinly spread guerrilla, it's easy to run around putting out fires and not pay enough attention to nonemergencies. You'll get better results if you focus on providing great customer service when you don't have to. Service when the customer is upset doesn't earn you many points. Doing the right thing by your customers when they *don't* expect it is the way to win.

Here are some ideas on ways to stay in touch with customers on a routine basis:

- Send a coupon for a discount on the next purchase. They've already bought from you once. Now you want to make them regular customers. So make it easy for them to buy from you again by offering them a special discount for previous customers only.

- Round off when making change. Even pennies are nothing to sneer at when you're trying to build up your profit margin. But investing a few cents or even a few dollars in a valuable customer may be the best use you can make of that spare change. Consider it a marketing expense.

- Send a potted plant to say thank you. You can set yourself apart by thanking your customers with a tangible reminder of how much you appreciate their business.

- Offer to stay open late if you sense a client is on a deadline. Don't wait for a special request. Many people won't ask because they're sure you could never accommodate them. If you realize that a customer is facing a crunch, volunteer your special attention at the most convenient time for them.

- If it's a small request from a big customer, do it for free. Sometimes free is the most profitable price for a small service or item. It's always unexpected, always appreciated, and will make you stand out in your customer's mind as gracious.

SOMETIMES YOU HAVE TO FIRE A CUSTOMER

Dave Wood made fine golf clubs by hand in his garage for years before a big distributor began to buy his clubs. But not long after he signed with the distributor, Dave canceled the pact, thus firing his biggest customer.

How can it be a good idea to get rid of some customers? Aren't customers our reason for being in business?

In Dave's case, the distributor wasn't being careful about where the clubs were sold, and the clubs began showing up in Tokyo pro shops. The gray market prices were undercutting Dave's loyal Japanese retailers in a very important market for him. Under the circumstances, firing his customer was a hole-in-one.

No matter how hard you try, some customers won't give you a fair shake. Some people abuse guarantees, returning pristine products with imaginary defects. Others demand special treatment, are rude to employees — and then buy from the guy across the street for a 10% discount. You don't need these customers.

Think we're kidding? Southwest Airlines has the best customer service record of any major airline. But when a customer mistreats employees or otherwise causes trouble, Southwest's one and only CEO, Herb Kelleher, sends a letter: "Fly somebody else."

One of the finest hotels in Canada keeps a list of customers who were

> One guerrilla travel agent we know took advantage of a recent commuter airplane scare. Rather than waiting to see what the FAA was going to decide about grounding certain commuter airlines, our guerrilla took the initiative to call all of his customers booked on upcoming flights. He made contingency plans for all of them and kept them apprised of the situation as new announcements were made. Some of his customers still canceled flights, but they were grateful that he had made such an effort to help them. His honesty, foresight, and quick action built customer loyalty and generated a lot of repeat business.

impossible to please. These ornery folk usually find that there's no room at the inn when they call for reservations.

Be careful here. The key is telling the difference between a merely demanding customer and one who isn't worth keeping. A business that is too quick to fire customers is probably going to be worse off than one that is too slow. So before you take the drastic step of firing a customer, try this four-step approach for dealing with problems.

1. Get the facts. Talk to the customer yourself. Find out exactly what the problem is or ask for an explanation of the behavior that's causing a problem.

2. Apologize for the problem. Even if it's the customer's fault, even if the customer won't see it your way, you must take responsibility. If you won't do this, don't even bother to try to fix the situation. You've already lost.

3. Propose a solution. Write it down for the customer. You may find that you're misunderstanding the customer's demands or that the customer is confused about the terms of your service. Usually it's easier to solve than you think.

4. Most important, do it. Fulfill your promised solution as you wrote it down. Keep the customer posted on your progress. When it's done, ask whether the customer is satisfied.

This approach isn't fail-safe. Some customers will take your determined effort to fix things as a sign of weakness and may refuse to participate in finding a solution. They may become even more demanding and unreasonable.

If that happens, fine. Your experimental solution has identified a problem customer. Next move: hand out the pink slip.

Once you've decided to fire a customer, think about damage control. It's bad enough to lose one sale. You don't want former customers bad-mouthing you all over town for the way you blew up at them.

Instead of letting your irritation show, choose a direct, businesslike tone and say, "I'm sorry, but it seems as though our business isn't going to be able to satisfy you. I'd like to suggest that you consider doing business elsewhere. You may want to consider some of these other businesses…"

Happily, it rarely comes to this. In all but a very few cases, a sincere effort to get the facts, express apologies, and come up with a solution will delight your customer. So go ahead and make a policy of outstanding customer service. Take a chance that your customers will appreciate it without exploiting you. Most of them will do just that.

TIP! The cost of keeping a customer is tiny compared to the cost of finding a new one. Consider customer service an investment.

3 WORD OF MOUTH
GENERATING A SALES FORCE OF CUSTOMERS

GUERRILLA ILLUSTRATOR STEVIE ANN RINEHART'S basic marketing tool operates according to what she calls "the concentric circle theory."

What's that?

Stevie explains that she began her home-based business by contacting her circle of family, friends, and business associates and telling them about her new endeavor. She gave them her brochure. She showed them samples of her work. She did some free work for those that needed it.

Those first few customers told their friends. The friends told some of their friends. The circle of people who knew about Stevie's fledgling business rapidly expanded to new circles.

Today she has enough business to devote herself full-time to Cardtoons by Stevie. But she still considers those concentric circles of satisfied, talkative customers her most effective marketing resource. They lead to more sales than brochures, direct mail pieces, or any of her other marketing tools.

By now you've realized Stevie's concentric circle theory is word-of-mouth marketing. Word of mouth and testimonials are the foundations of guerrilla marketing. They make the most of the one-to-one, relationship-building focus of all guerrilla marketing strategies.

WHY YOU SHOULD CARE ABOUT WORD OF MOUTH

Studies have shown that every time a customer is dissatisfied, she'll complain to an average of nine people. A satisfied customer, on the other hand, will tell just one other person about what a great job you did. That means you've got to generate nine times as many happy customers as dissatisfied ones just to stay even.

A neighbor, friend, or co-worker recommending a product or service is the most credible marketer there is because, in our age of media overload and marketing hype, the one thing you can't buy is word of mouth. And consumers recognize this. The single most important element in generating a buying decision is now word of mouth.

"Great," you say. "Word of mouth is the most potent, most effective form of marketing, but I can't magically make it happen." Not true. You *can* create word of mouth. You can plan it and enjoy its benefits when your plans come to fruition.

There are two parts to word of mouth for guerrillas: referrals and testimonials.

REFERRALS: THE BEST WORD OF MOUTH

Referrals are the guerrilla's best friend. A referral is the positive last step in the word-of-mouth process — when a satisfied customer tells a friend to do business with you. Any decent business is bound to create customers who will attract new customers. But sometimes your customers don't just tell their friends: they beg, they cajole, they take the prospect by the hand and bring him to you. These customers cross the line and become zealots — every guerrilla's dream.

If you do your homework, you can create a cadre of word-of-mouth specialists. You've probably been one of them yourself. Most of us have a favorite restaurant or pizza parlor where we take friends. "You've got to try this — it's the best pastrami sandwich in this hemisphere!" No matter that your friend hates pastrami. You're on a mission to spread the word about this place.

Passionate people push more than restaurants and delis. Run into someone who uses a Macintosh and you're sure to get an earful. Or someone who skis regularly at Aspen. Or an executive who drives a Lexus. We're pleased to say that there are also quite a few guerrilla marketing zealots out there. Many of the people who buy one of the books in the series do so because a friend, banker, co-worker, or spouse

 TIP! At the end of a sales call, ask the prospect (whether he bought or not) for three leads on other people who might be interested. Bang! You'll never need to make another cold call.

recommended it. We hope that by the time you finish this book, you'll become one of them.

People want to help their friends. They also want to demonstrate that they're clever shoppers, having discovered the perfect source for a given product or service. And customers can be grateful and savvy. If a business is special, they want to reward it, help it thrive, make sure it's still in business the next time they need it.

HOW TO GENERATE WORD OF MOUTH

How do you build referrals? How do you transform ordinary happy customers into extraordinary word-of-mouth zealots, people on a mission to help you succeed? By taking these four steps:

1. Overdeliver.

2. Make it easy to refer.

3. Reward the zealots.

4. Ask for help.

Wow Your Customers by Overdelivering.

Quality products and attentive customer service are the best marketing tools available at any price. There's no better way to generate word of mouth. Impress a customer beyond her expectations and she'll tell five of her friends, not just one.

We have already discussed customer service in detail. But some aspects of service are especially effective at generating word of mouth, and they are worth repeating here.

1. Expedite delivery. Time is the most precious commodity for many businesses and individuals. If you can speed up the processing and delivery of every purchase beyond the customer's expectations, you will be in an excellent position to ask for and get a testimonial. If people expect to get a pizza in forty-five minutes, do it in ten minutes. If your competitor generates freelance articles in a week, offer yours in one day.

 TIP! A testimonial with a very unspecific source can backfire on you. If a testimonial in your brochure is from "a client in Dobbs Ferry, N.Y.," it won't have nearly the impact of one from "John Joseph, President of Acme Automobiles." The first looks as if you had to manufacture it. But John Joseph stood up and endorsed you.

2. Provide personal service. Personal attention is the guerrilla's stock in trade. If you make your customer feel special, he'll want to reciprocate. Discover ways to make customers members of the family. At the very least, remember their names, their habits, and their birthdays.

3. Answer questions. Teach your clients how to live without you. Pay attention to their legitimate queries and answer them honestly and quickly. A guerrilla who's always trying to save clients money is sure to be cherished — and mentioned a lot.

4. Handle complaints. Nobody likes criticism. But it's a mistake to avoid hearing complaints, valid or otherwise. If you handle a complaint promptly, courteously, and fully, you'll give a customer a real reason to testify about your service. And don't go halfway. Go overboard. If your late delivery cost the client money, don't offer a simple refund. Give him three free replacements. If a part breaks, don't hassle the client about fifty cents. Insist on fixing it yourself, now, at no charge. Arguing always leads to one fewer customer and lots of negative word of mouth.

5. Solve problems. A dry cleaner who thoughtfully replaces missing buttons is doing more than he was hired to do, but he is building a relationship that can turn a customer into a zealot. If you write for a magazine, send the editor story leads or competitive news he may not have heard or seen.

6. Stay in touch. You know by now that it's much easier to sell to a happy customer. Talking to your best customers regularly is a great way to make them feel like family. Remember, you're not calling to sell anything today. Instead, you're laying the foundation for a more profitable relationship in the future.

7. Concentrate on long-term relationships. Some 20% of your customers are going to generate 80% of your referrals. Identify the potential zealots and never let them go.

8. Forgo a sale if it's not right for the customer. Remember, you're involved with key customers for the long haul. So when you refuse to sell something that won't solve the problem, they appreciate that you

 TIP! Buy a leather notebook and have your best testimonials laminated for insertion. When making sales calls, hand the notebook to your prospects and suggest they page through it.

are placing their interests ahead of your own. That's so rare in business, it's a powerful motivation for them to say nice things about you.

Make It Easy.

Great word of mouth can be encouraged. Stevie the cartoonist uses certain techniques to make it easy for her clients to become zealots.

She prints her name and phone number on the back of each greeting card she designs. People get one of her cards from a friend (an implicit endorsement), turn the card over, see her number, and call.

She includes at least two business cards in every brochure she mails. One is for the recipient. The second is to be given to a friend or colleague who might be interested in her work.

Carmine's is a New York restaurant that's jammed almost every night. Unfortunately, it doesn't accept reservations for parties of less than six. Want dinner at Carmine's? You'd better find five friends with a taste for Italian food, or be prepared to wait. This built-in referral engine turns every satisfied Carmine's customer into a salesperson trying to track down five more new customers.

> Dawn Orford, a home-based trade show consultant, sends a follow-up survey to each client after she completes a job. With a 90% return rate, the surveys have turned into a great way to generate testimonials. As a result, Dawn can send a sheet full of testimonials to every prospective client.

Reward the Zealots.

A good referral is a great benefit to your business. Why not give your customers some positive feedback for referring customers to you?

Offer existing customers discounts, gift certificates, gifts, accessories, special sale notifications, or free services for sending you business. It doesn't have to be a formal program, and it shouldn't seem like a bribe. But there's nothing wrong with your showing gratitude.

Guerrilla Jan Melnik gives customers who refer others a coupon good for a discount on future secretarial services. She places no restrictions on the offer. Is it risky? Well, one customer has referred so much business to her that he hasn't had to pay Jan since the first time he hired her. (If that's risky, Jan is fearless.)

How about Christian Beal of ReComp? A guerrilla who sells refurbished Macintosh computers out of his apartment in Florida, he sends a letter asking customers for five referrals one week after they have purchased from him. If a customer returns the completed form, Chris mails him a popular shareware program. If one of the referrals buys a computer system from ReComp, then Chris sends the original customer a $25 check.

Keeping track of whom to reward is simple. One way is to code your brochures. Then, ask prospective customers for the code on their brochure. Or use the old standby: "How did you hear about us?"

Ask for Help.

Often, customers don't realize how important word of mouth is to your business, so sometimes you have to ask for help. Your business may be too specialized or your customers too isolated for word of mouth and testimonials to occur naturally. You can step in and act as a middleman.

Ever buy life insurance? Insurance companies have long relied on personal referrals to generate leads. That's why the agent who sold you your policy asked for the names of three people you knew before the ink was dry on your policy. Referrals of this sort generate the best leads and highest closing rates.

At the time of a sale, suggest "If you enjoyed your experience with us, please tell a friend." What have you got to lose? It works even better to put it in writing. Send a letter to customers asking them to talk up your company.

Ask your clients to send your product or service as a gift. A massage therapist with twenty regular clients could offer half-price (or free) gift certificates to her best customers. Every gift turns into an audition before a potential new customer.

Magazines do this all the time. A good proportion of those little pieces of paper that fall out of the pages of your favorite magazine are for a gift subscription to give to a friend. Restaurants do it, too, pitching gift certificates around the holiday season.

TESTIMONIALS

A zealot is a marketer's dream. But even the most determined zealot can't reach more than a few dozen prospects.

Word of mouth that goes beyond a personal recommendation and becomes a public, explicit endorsement is a testimonial. Generally, testimonials are written, although they can also be aural (on the radio), visual (on TV), or live (a personal appearance).

Think of the last time a customer complimented you. Could it have been a testimonial? Chances are, yes. Keep your eyes and ears open, and you'll find testimonials all around. Here are three places to check:

1. Letters. There's nothing like a statement from a hard-nosed business-man on his letterhead stating that you are the greatest thing since sliced bread. It's hard copy. It's credible. It's in black and white. Gather such precious communications in a laminated notebook and don't hesitate to pull it out when you talk to a prospect. Say something like, "As you can see, our customers love our service. I hope that after we've done some work for you, you'll send us a letter as well."

2. Conversation. It's common to brush off compliments from customers in a conversation. Go ahead. Be modest. But don't forget those com-pliments. Many can easily be used as testimonials. Jot them down while you're talking or soon after. They're too valuable to be lost.

3. Surveys. Many surveys ask for respondents' impressions of your busi-ness. Unfortunately, when tabulating survey results, these mini-essays tend to be ignored because they are not neat, like numbers. Don't make that mistake. Look over the commentary and keep the gems as testimonials.

Ask for Testimonials.

If you sit back and wait, testimonials will eventually come in. But if you seek them out, you'll get them now. What are you waiting for?

Try saying: "We're very happy that you've enjoyed doing business with us. Would you be willing to go on record as recommending us?"

Or send out a customer survey that, along with other questions, includes a direct request for a testimonial. This gives you a chance to put your query in writing and allows customers time to decide in private.

You might say: "Like all of our interactions with you, we will keep survey results confidential. But if you feel our service has been excep-tional, we'd consider it a personal favor if you would enclose a letter reflecting this that we could show to prospective customers. Thanks."

Another way to create a high-impact testimonial is to swap promo-tion or publicity for a testimonial. American Express has a long-running ad campaign in which CEOs of businesses large and small mention their use of the card. What motivates Charles Lazarus of Toys "R" Us to talk up American Express? Could it be the millions of dollars of free adver-tising his stores get from the campaign?

TIP! Offer existing customers a discount for every new client they refer.

Find the Right Person for a Testimonial.

The best place to look is on your own customer list. But if you're just starting out, you might need to jump ahead a few rungs, seek out a credible source or two, and actively turn them into legitimate zealots. How do you do that?

Use "six degrees of separation." It's said that you are separated from every other person on earth by only six mutual acquaintances. If you ask a friend if she has any friends who know any well-known people who could be persuaded by a personal appeal to endorse your business... well, you're halfway to anybody in the world. Make testimonial-seeking a regular part of your networking and see what happens.

Another tactic to try is hooking up with a charity. People who would never dream of selling their endorsements give them away free to charities and to businesses associated with those charities. Some organizations will swap an endorsement from a celebrity backer for a contribution or other help from your business.

Work the Influence Pyramid.

Now that you can transform customers into zealots, think about which zealots do you the most good.

In almost every industry and every neighborhood, there's a pyramid of influence. For example, in the computer business, there are about 250 editors, pundits, corporate buyers, and retailers who are the opinion leaders for the millions of people who will eventually buy the technology. These are the people who brand a product "hot" or "tired." Microsoft has done an extraordinary job of wooing these influencers with obvious success.

The pyramid works everywhere, not just in large high-tech industries. Officials of trade groups, professional associations, community organizations, and fraternal societies know lots of people in specific target markets. Get one or two of them as satisfied customers and they can be the source of your best referrals.

Christian Beal of ReComp concentrates a lot of his marketing efforts on making sales that will leverage his time and effort in the future. He recently sold a computer system to the president of a parent-teacher organization. She referred ReComp to her daughter's elementary school.

 Send your customers something when they least expect it. One guerrilla we know mails lottery tickets to her best customers every time the jackpot hits $5 million. This unusual gesture generates a lot of goodwill and keeps her customers talking about her.

Christian now has the opportunity to sell sixteen computers to the school. One contact, seventeen sales. That's not bad.

Home-based business plan writer Marcia Layton spends a lot of time cultivating a variety of financial consultants, bankers, lawyers, and venture capitalists — anyone who recommends services to entrepreneurs.

By staying in touch, she doesn't mean calling up and saying "hi." Marcia always has a reason to call, write, or fax. For example, if she writes a business plan for a client she knows is looking for capital, she will write an "executive summary" of the plan and send it to a variety of capital sources. Even if the source is not interested in investing in the business, he appreciates the favor and keeps Marcia in mind as the person who wrote the plan. Indeed, several of her "executive summaries" have turned into new business for her.

MAKE THE BEST USE OF TESTIMONIALS

Before you start plastering testimonials all over town, take a few minutes to follow some common-sense strategy to save time and hassle later.

To make the most of a testimonial, you have to be able to use it freely. Naturally, people may be concerned about how you're going to use it. They may even change their minds about it afterward. Protect yourself by having customers sign a release form that states exactly how you will (and will not) use their testimonial.

Presentation counts. Sometimes it's not *what* was said but *how* it was said. If your testimonials are displayed as yellowing scraps of paper tacked on a bulletin board, you're wasting much of their potential impact. Here are seven ways to present testimonials and referrals that will leverage them into guerrilla marketing powerhouses:

1. Use letterhead. A company's letterhead carries a major identification message, so ask for the testimonial on letterhead and you're likely to get it.

2. Print a booklet. If all your sales are made in personal calls, spend some money and have the testimonials professionally laminated in a notebook.

3. Use them in ads. Movie theaters, booksellers, and software publishers are just a few of the businesses that rely heavily on advertised testimonials from professional critics. Testimonials from a variety of sources can be used in other businesses as well. The best ad testimonials include pictures of the people endorsing you.

4. Give individual customer profiles. You have credibility because your customers know and relate to you personally. The people who give you testimonials will also benefit from a little exposure. Many successful marketers make their testimonial-givers seem human and appealing by giving personal details about them in ads.

Think of the long-running "Dewar's Profiles" series of ads from Dewar's Scotch. Apple Computer has gotten raves for its "What I Have on My PowerBook" ads, which describe the recipes, half-written novels, and to-do lists that celebrities and ordinary people keep on their laptop computers.

5. List your clients. Sometimes there is more strength in numbers than details. Seeing a long list of your past and present satisfied clients gives prospective customers a good feeling about your business. They think, "If all these other people have worked with her, I'm not likely to get burned. At the very least, this will help justify my decision to go with her." It's human nature, and it can be used to your advantage.

6. Give telephone contacts. You'll need permission from past clients, but it's probably worth asking. There's nothing more convincing than hearing from a live person that the decision you are about to make is a good one.

7. Focus on testimonials. Devote a page or section of your brochure to them. Pick any three business books from your shelf. Notice how the back cover and one or more inside pages are devoted to testimonials? Superselling business author Harvey Mackay invests not just one but fifteen pages (!) of one of his books to testimonials from dozens of well-known people. *The Guerrilla Marketing Handbook* devotes the very first page to more than a dozen rave reviews, and there are two more on the back cover.

The back panel of guerrilla Pattianne Turner's brochure for her home-based Computer Aided Services & Training business is devoted to some compelling testimonials. One says: "Ms. Turner's work proves to be of exceptional quality and I would recommend her services to any-

 TIP! Be careful when you edit endorsements and testimonials. If you offend the customer who gave you the endorsement, you'll do real damage to the relationship. Take a minute to run the edited testimonial by the satisfied customer. They'll generally give you an okay, and they'll be grateful for being consulted.

one. — Maria Erdmann-Raddatz, Chartered Accountant." Doing the same with your testimonials can be invaluable.

If you don't contact your customers with printed materials, don't use written testimonials. Use voice testimonials in radio ads and on-hold messages. Obtain oral testimonials by tape-recording customers praising you.

Make your testimonials relevant. Remember when, at the height of his football fame, Joe Namath posed for an ad in pantyhose? Remember what brand he was advertising? Neither do we.

Help turn wishy-washy compliments into punchy, hard-hitting referrals. Recently, a doctor referred a surgeon to us because he was a nice person. That's not what we were looking for! A referral indicating the surgeon's skill, number of patients, and base hospital would have been more likely to make us go see him.

Help your clients write powerful testimonials by showing them examples. Then they can make sure the one they are writing for you is useful.

Try to echo your other marketing messages in word of mouth and testimonials. If you're "The South's Premier Package Designer," a useful testimonial could be "I looked everywhere below the Mason-Dixon Line before I finally found your company — one I could count on."

How much is a testimonial worth? About as much as the person giving it. Identify testimonial-givers fully. If you don't tell your customers and prospects who is giving a testimonial, that part of the value remains a question mark.

We've all seen testimonials signed "H.N., Los Angeles." Not very convincing, is it? H.N. could be an expert or an ignoramus. Even worse is the use of completely unsigned testimonials. Without a name, a testimonial is just a slogan. With a name, it's an endorsement.

A testimonial in Pattianne Turner's brochure starts off: "A major part of the success of our Grand Opening was due to Turner." It continues: "Ms. Turner's exceptional skills in the design of our menus, gift certificates, and advertising provided us with affordable quality work."

Nice, huh? And it ends: "Dwayne Wilson, owner, Cathedral

 TIP! Community involvement is a good way to generate word-of-mouth advertising. Sponsor a Little League team or a food drive for the homeless. Donate your services to a charity auction or offer to provide your service for free to a nonprofit organization.

Quarters Restaurant." Notice the full name and title of the person giving the testimonial. This complete identification increases the credibility of a testimonial tenfold.

Of course you won't forget to say thank you. You're a guerrilla!

TIP! The single best way to generate word-of-mouth advertising is to amaze your customers on a regular basis!

4 PUBLICITY
FREE ADVERTISING FOR THE HOME-BASED GUERRILLA

LIKE EVERYBODY ELSE IN the crafts and hobbies business, Donna Hawley was advertising in places like *Country Sampler* magazine. Her ads generated initial sales for her new doll-designing business, Hawley House, but they didn't help her stand out from the crowd. What she needed was something different than just another ad, something with greater credibility and prominence.

Publicity was the answer. A true guerrilla marketer, she first carefully selected her goal, then patiently cultivated personal contacts. Finally, she made a detailed, narrowly targeted, perfectly timed proposal to get what she wanted.

The result? A photo of one of her designs on the cover of *Country Sampler*. The targeted audience of hobbyists and collectors was a perfect match with her business. Even better, her professional reputation got a boost she couldn't have obtained any other way.

As Donna's experience shows, publicity is one of the marketing arenas where the home-based guerrilla's unique traits can be used to best advantage. It requires careful positioning, intensive study, and prolonged follow-through. Above all, publicity is a field where the personal touch pays off. A guerrilla who does it right will discover one of the lowest-cost, highest-impact marketing methods available.

PUBLIC RELATIONS VS. PUBLICITY

Publicity is part of the broader field of public relations. Often called PR, it is the art and science of affecting what people think about you and your business. It can help you break out of obscurity, guide you away from trouble, and even aid you in emergencies. It can include everything from how you handle customer complaints to your reputation with regulators in Washington.

Everyone has PR, whether or not they actively pay for it. Libya and Iraq have bad PR, while Switzerland enjoys a great reputation. Kodak has cultivated an image as a caring member of your family, while Dow Chemical, which does not make as many chemicals as Kodak, gets more negative PR.

The Pentium computer chip — and its bugs — became a PR nightmare for computer giant Intel when it did not take sufficient responsibility for the problem. Within a few short weeks, several hundred million dollars of image advertising went down the drain. The public began to believe that Intel was callous and not particularly careful about the way it manufactured its product.

Ben Cohen and Jerry Greenfield of Ben & Jerry's generated good PR by running a contest to pick the new CEO of their company. Their creative promotion attracted national attention and reinforced the company's image as community-oriented and fun-loving — the right image to have if you are in the ice cream business.

Taking control of your public relations is a vital element of every guerrilla plan. Even if you're not as big as Intel or Ben & Jerry's, you still live and die by the public's perception of you and your business. In that sense, PR is tied in with almost everything else discussed in this book. It's a golden chance for your size and position as a home-based business to make the public perceive your company as run by a real person, not by a faceless bureaucracy.

One of the most direct ways to influence your public relations is through publicity. People generally believe the media are impartial and truthful, so anything reported in a news article goes a long way toward building your public persona. In this chapter, you will learn how to generate publicity that helps credibility, encourages word of mouth, and opens doors that you could never reach with advertising alone.

WHAT IS PUBLICITY?

Publicity is the process of getting your name to appear in the news media. Unlike advertising, publicity aims to bring you to the attention of the media, with the goal of getting yourself interviewed, quoted, or even featured in a story.

Publicity is a marketing tool custom-made for guerrillas. It isn't about who has the biggest advertising budget (lots of big companies get lousy publicity). Instead, it's about carefully selecting and studying a small number of highly targeted media outlets that give you access to the majority of your potential and existing customers. These are precisely the advantages that successful guerrilla publicists like Jan Melnik bring to all their marketing efforts.

Jan, the home-based owner of Comprehensive Services, Plus, in Durham, Connecticut, relies on building relationships with nearby writers and editors to keep her business growing steadily. In 1991 she targeted the lifestyle editor of her local paper. After following her stories for months, Jan understood what she was and wasn't interested in. Jan then called the editor and pitched the fact that she was working at home with three young children, two of them twins. The newspaper ran a story about the "mother of twins" club that Jan had started. Although the article didn't focus on her business, the photo used was taken in her home office. The caption mentioned her business and the story included what Jan did and who her clients were.

Since then, Jan has cultivated relationships with several other local business editors. She stays in constant contact with them and even takes them out to lunch to discuss story ideas. She views her media contacts as friends and treats them as such. Jan's persistent publicity efforts have resulted in her business's being featured twice on the front page of a major section of two large local newspapers. These stories resulted in a lot of new business.

Publicity alone does not equal a marketing effort, however. For one thing, there's too little control. You can order an advertisement to run on a particular day to coincide with your business needs. But you can't decide when an article will be published or even if it will be published. You can't tell the reporter what to say about you. Nor can you get your message repeated at regular intervals for a long period of time, a basic principle of advertising.

Publicity can also be unpredictable. Marcia Yudkin, the author of *Six Steps to Free Publicity*, recalls the time she carefully researched and wrote a press release about her business and sent it to more than a hundred highly targeted media contacts. Ordinarily, her release would probably have generated interest, but the Gulf War broke out the day after she mailed it, so it was largely ignored. On the other hand, a simple letter

TIP! Sure-fire way to get press coverage: Do a survey or run a contest and turn the results into a press release.

> Offer something for free or at a discount in your press release. When Barbara Brabec first published *Homemade Money*, she targeted much of her publicity campaign at *Family Circle* magazine. All of her efforts were ignored until she sent a release that offered an exclusive "home-business information package" to the magazine's readers for $1. Suddenly Barbara received coverage that resulted in 10,000 inquiries.

and a copy of her newsletter mailed to an editor resulted in a story in the *Maine Sunday Telegram*.

Publicity is cheaper in the long run and better at building credibility than advertising alone. When you appear in a news story, you don't get a bill. And that kind of exposure can establish you as a reliable expert in your field far more effectively than any advertising campaign.

What about the risk of negative coverage? Actually, it's far smaller than most of us realize. It may seem that a lot of news is negative. The fact is Woodward and Bernstein, who broke the Watergate Scandal, were exceptions. Most reporters aren't scoop-hungry investigators. They're wage earners who want to please their editors with as little effort as possible, and they're happy to let you provide them with ideas and facts for publishable stories. That is why most publicity is positive for people and their businesses.

You're still not convinced? Go to the library and glance through a few days' issues of several newspapers, including the *Wall Street Journal, USA Today*, and some local papers. You'll discover that the same stories appear over and over again. That's because they were initiated by the companies being covered, not by an eager young reporter out looking for a scoop.

PUBLICITY PLUSES

There are three reasons that it's absolutely essential that you make publicity part of your guerrilla marketing arsenal.

News Reports Influence People.

A century ago, the publisher William Randolph Hearst used his rabble-rousing newspapers to drag the U.S. into the Spanish-American War. They're not causing wars anymore, but newspapers still wield influence today.

People also remember what they read in a news report far longer than they do ad copy. And if you're lucky enough to be quoted, they're going to remember that you are an authority, someone with genuine stature.

Retention, prestige, influence — PR packs a lot of punch. Favorable publicity in a top forum like *Consumer Reports* or the *Today* show — as well as many smaller outlets that are equally influential in their niches — can literally make your business overnight in a way that no amount of advertising can.

Dollar for Dollar, It's the Most Cost-Effective Communication.

Take a typical trade journal with a circulation of 25,000 and a basic rate of $2,500 for a one-time, full-page ad. If you sell to businesses in that industry, you're going to want to be there. You can plunk down your $2,500 and run your ad — once. Or you can embark on a focused, long-term publicity campaign to ensure that your business is regularly featured in the very same journal.

Look at how Donna Hawley got Hawley House on the cover of a perfectly targeted publication. That space isn't for sale at any price! Yet her investment was essentially nothing. Instead of cash, she spent the time selecting the right market, carefully studying it, and producing a distinctive pitch with a better likelihood of success.

Publicity Works with, Rather Than Limits, Your Other Marketing.

Good publicity is an excellent way to leverage and increase the impact of all your marketing efforts, from direct mail to networking to generating word-of-mouth advertising.

Cut out and copy articles about your company and include them with anything you send to prospective customers. Use them in brochures, as signs, in press kits, and as framed display pieces in your office. Yesterday's newspaper is dead and gone, but its story can — and should — live on forever.

Take advantage of the credibility you gain by appearing in the press as an expert in your field. Keep the momentum going by offering to speak at conferences and trade shows, to local organizations, and even to students.

Remember Jan Melnik of Comprehensive Services, Plus? The media coverage she has received over the years has certainly given her business credibility. Beyond that, it has allowed her to enter new markets with new products that meet her customers' needs. As the result of one article, she began receiving calls from people who wanted her advice on starting their own business. Jan started a consulting service and now not only provides her clients with printed materials but advises them in other aspects of home business startup.

GETTING STARTED: MAKING YOUR PUBLICITY PLAN

As a guerrilla, all your marketing efforts must be highly focused on results. Therefore, before you make a single move to generate publicity, you need a plan. There are many different ways to achieve different kinds of publicity in different places. Unless you know exactly what you want your publicity to accomplish, you're likely to be disappointed.

Start by asking yourself what you want and need to get from publicity.

Why Do You Want Publicity?

Publicity is too time-consuming to pursue just for ego gratification or because your mother-in-law will be impressed. There should be a solid business reason for publicity. It's highly effective at creating credibility, increasing name recognition, and building relationships. Which of these goals does your business need?

When Loveda and Tim Finley of Columbus, Ohio, started selling family safety equipment door-to-door, they desperately needed credibility in the affluent residential areas they had targeted. After waging an effective publicity campaign, they were quoted in several local newspaper stories on family safety. Their reputations as safety experts grew, providing just the entrée they needed.

Who Do You Want to Reach?

Once you know your market, you can determine which media outlets you need to focus on. If your business is writing résumés for local college graduates, it makes sense to pursue coverage in the business sections of the local and college newspapers.

James Brown, a former FBI agent, sells telephone systems to city police departments through Carlton Security Systems, which is based in his Indianapolis home. He could try to get an interview on the local radio station or a mention in the *Indianapolis Star*, but it probably wouldn't do his business much good. He should target his efforts toward gaining publicity in the *Police Chief* and *Police and Security News*, the publications police officers are most likely to read.

It's tempting for any guerrilla to consider the entire world as a potential market. But be realistic. Most of your sales will come from just a few

TIP! A personalized press release is often more effective. Highlight the relevant paragraphs or jot a note in the margin to an editor you have worked with before.

sources. Effort expended elsewhere won't be as effective. That's why it's important to decide where you want publicity before you start.

What Kind of Publicity Do You Want?

The kind of publicity James Brown got would be worthless to someone like Donna Hawley. She sells to a narrowly targeted group of well-informed consumers all over the country. For her, name recognition and a way to break through the competition are critical. Being featured in a highly prominent magazine cover illustration was just what she needed.

If you need credentials, you want to be quoted as an expert. If you need to explain the benefits of a complex product or service, a feature article about you by a knowledgeable reporter can be invaluable in developing your market. If all you need is name recognition, on the other hand, prominent placement on the cover of the right trade journal may be what you're after.

What Are Your Goals?

There are as many ways to measure the success of a publicity campaign as there are media outlets and guerrilla publicists. You may decide that you want a number of feature stories profiling your business in several distinct outlets. Or you could aim to get a single magazine feature in your specific industry's trade journal.

If no one in your field has ever appeared on the cover of *Forbes*, it's probably not worth pursuing too aggressively. Editors aren't usually interested in stretching the boundaries of their publications, and you'll be a lot more efficient if you focus on the achievable.

Ask yourself what you want your publicity to accomplish. Do you want to generate sales or are you trying to find the best leads and position yourself as an expert in your field? Either way, you should have a specific objective for your campaign before you lift a finger or pick up a phone.

When Sandra Beckwith, the home-based publisher of "The Do(o) Little Report," began her newsletter 52

in April 1993, she set her sights on the media as her primary means of generating subscribers. She outlined her objectives, strategies, and the challenges she might face getting the press to cover her in the right light. The result? She far exceeded her goal of generating 1,000 inquiries in six months. During the first ten months of her campaign, Sandra had 15,000 inquiries. She spent less than $5,000 and received over $4.5 million of coverage!

What Is Your Time Frame?

Now that you have answered *what*, you need to address *when*. Once you've decided to seek publicity, it's tempting to sit down at your computer and fire off a few letters. Don't. One-shot press releases rarely work. Odds are, the reporters you contact have never heard of you. A story about an unknown quantity is hard to sell to an editor and even harder to make interesting to busy readers. You need to start by engaging in regular and frequent communication with your target media outlets so that they become familiar with you and your business.

Plan your publicity a year in advance and pay attention to lead times. Most trade journals and monthly magazines need at least two months' notice. That means the press release you send in December does not turn into a story until February or March — a little late for your special Christmas promotion.

Every month, send out a new press release. The first release may get tossed in the round file. The second may also. But gradually your name will become familiar to the journalist you are pitching. Eventually, a perfectly tuned pitch or a slow news day will make that journalist pick up the phone and call you.

Here's a sample plan for a guerrilla in the package design industry:

Date Sent	Date Run	Topic
January	April	Free research report available in February
February	March	New clients announced
March	June	Results of exclusive survey of executives available in April
April	May	Nominations announced for best package designs of the year (we hope!)
May	September	New packaging pricing software out in June
June	July	New hire announced
July	August	New clients announced
August	December	Top Christmas gifts for executives in the packaging industry
September	January	Profile of Joe Guerrilla — his tenth anniversary in the biz
October	November	Article on the evils of recycling mania
November	December	Packaging pros pick the best packages of the year

Notice how suggestions with a short shelf life, such as new client announcements, are slotted for publication soon after the release. These releases will be pitched to packaging trade journals and local business and daily newspapers. The Christmas gift idea is presented in July, when many magazine editors are planning December issues.

Some of your ideas should have timeless appeal. The piece on recycling's downside, for instance, would be relevant at almost any time, so it can be pitched months ahead of the expected publication date. Editors appreciate ideas that they can file away for emergencies. Stories that are not time bound can fill unexpected gaps, when another story doesn't work out.

Jeff Mayer is a home-based consultant in executive organization. A publicity hound, he stays in constant contact with the media, calling at regular intervals and sending out press releases almost every month. One release was full of organization tips. Although nothing came of it immediately, one reporter called Jeff six months later and wrote a nice feature story on corporate organizing, quoting him as an expert in the field.

PATIENCE PAYS

Your publicity will be most successful if you make it a standard part of your business. Ilise Benun, a Hoboken, New Jersey, consultant in self-promotion and marketing, publicizes her business constantly with a quarterly newsletter called "The Art of Self-Promotion." Most people have to pay for it. But she sends it free to more than a hundred press contacts with an invitation to excerpt anything they find useful — attributing Ilise of course.

Not surprisingly, Ilise has been quoted in a wide variety of publications as an expert on self-promotion. The media contacts also help her locate opportunities to write her own articles — an even better way to build expert credentials. Readers often offer her consulting jobs and speaking engagements and buy still more subscriptions to the newsletter.

Ilise's publicity program succeeds in part because it's regular, predictable, and solid. Four times a year, like clockwork, a large group of media people receive her newsletter. They can hardly help but accept that she's for real, knowledgeable, and experienced in her field. She may always have been just as qualified; the point is that it takes time to get the message across.

So you're armed with a plan. You've answered *what* and *when*. Now it's time to determine *Who*.

 TIP! Although TV coverage may seem attractive, the majority of home-based businesses benefit most from press coverage. Print lasts, and it's easier to put a clipping in your book of testimonials.

WHERE TO FOCUS YOUR PUBLICITY EFFORTS

There are more than 9,500 magazines and newsletters published in the U.S., more than 1,100 commercial TV stations, and about 1,600 daily newspapers. A single mid-size city by itself will have twenty or so radio stations. These numbers don't include countless other potential outlets, such as nationwide clear-channel radio stations, community newspapers, and cable television.

There are clearly too many outlets for you to cover them all. That's why a critical early step in your publicity strategy is to identify those places you'd like your business to be covered. Don't try to pitch your stories to everyone. Instead, select a relatively small number of the news outlets that are most likely to be receptive and beneficial.

Where will you make your pitch? The answer depends on your marketing position statement and your target market. It's tempting to select, say, *Newsweek, 60 Minutes,* and maybe the *Wall Street Journal* and figure you've done your job. But don't let your ego get in the way here.

Are you "the Valley's Only All-Natural Garden Service"? If so, your ideal media outlet will be local and have a large audience among gardening enthusiasts. Possibilities include the gardening column of your local newspaper and a local-access channel gardening show.

We'd all like to see a glowing testimonial on the cover of *Time,* but would that really be more effective than a profile in the *Valley Times* home section or *Environmental Gardeners' Digest?* Maybe not, and the odds of success with the smaller publications are incalculably higher.

Business information specialist Kimberly Stanséll is proud that her target press list is actually *smaller* these days than when she began four years ago. She started with a general press list and mass-mailed her press releases, often with little result. Since then, she has narrowed down her list to the publications that seem to fit her needs the best and editors and writers with whom she has been able to build relationships. Now, when she mails out a press release, the percentage of people who respond is three times higher than it once was.

Marcia Layton, a home-based business plan writer, maintains a list of her top twenty media contacts, a mixture of national magazines and trade publications. Each is highly targeted, either directly at her clients or at people who provide her with business referrals. Her list includes major magazines like *Entrepreneur* and *Home Office Computing* as well as targeted trade publications like *Your Company* (an American Express publication sent to small business owners) and the *Journal of Commercial Finance.* She sends out a new press release almost every month and never fails to get at least one response.

Whom should you target? Make a list of the ten types of people you'd most like to read an article about your product or service. What do they read? Whom do they trust? What's the most effective way to reach these people? If you don't know, ask a few of your customers which newspapers they read, newsletters they subscribe to, and broadcasts they listen to or watch. Select a target group of four or five outlets to start.

DO YOUR HOMEWORK

For your publicity to succeed, you have to learn to think like a news-

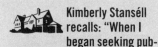 Kimberly Stanséll recalls: "When I began seeking publicity, I used media directories at my local library to create a media list. As I began to receive responses to my releases, I developed a special list of contacts. Developing a special list helps you move away from sending so many press releases to blind contacts. So now, rather than sending 500 releases to people I don't know, the majority of my mailings go to people and outlets who are acquainted with me or whom I have developed a rapport with. The result: an increased chance for a placement."

hound. Take your target list and head to the library for some research. Read the last four or five issues of each publication you are targeting. If you're going after a broadcast outlet, listen to or watch a few shows. Take notes and make copies of articles, especially any that look as though they may have been generated by a news release.

Note which writers or reporters are getting the most bylines. Select busy, active journalists whose stories tend to be positive and upbeat and similar in content to the ideas you are trying to pitch.

Now you should have a list of ten names — perhaps a couple for each of your target outlets. Think of your target newshounds as another group of customers. Your job is to look at what they've used in the past, figure out what they need, and provide it.

Most reporters and editors want a story that will get maximum play for minimum effort. That means a subject that is interesting to the largest possible number of the potential audience, out of the ordinary, but not so arcane that it requires a lot of difficult research.

As a home-based guerrilla, you are in the unique position of being able to provide such stories. Jeff Mayer, the home-based executive organization consultant in Chicago, is an expert on a subject that most reporters are not. And many people appreciate the type of advice that he can give. So when Jeff approaches the media, he has story suggestions with built-in appeal, already thoroughly and credibly researched. The combination has added up to scores of interviews for Jeff and invaluable publicity for Mayer Enterprises.

KEEP IN TOUCH

Building personal relationships plays a key role here. Once you make a media contact, keep in touch. Don't just call when you've got something to sell. Don't miss an opportunity to maximize your strengths as a home-based business while eliminating competition from larger, impersonal organizations.

Jan Melnik builds relationships by keeping in touch with her press contacts. She takes them to lunch to pitch new story ideas or simply asks their advice on a particular problem her business is facing. She also acknowledges reporters who write about her with a nice handwritten note and sometimes a potted plant. Occasionally she even sends a letter to the reporter's boss, saying what a great job the writer did. Her efforts help to keep her relationships with the media alive.

DEVELOPING NEWSY IDEAS

Now it's time for the creative part. Go back to your list of ten media contacts. Given what you have learned about their reporting, can you think of stories featuring your business that they might cover?

The sample publicity plan shown earlier gives you an idea of the kinds of stories to generate. It's a mix of the mundane, like the new hires, and the marvelous, like the contrarian piece on recycling. That's the way it ought to be. Not every story will cause fistfights on street corners. Your business will also have routine news it needs to get out, and editors want to publish that as well.

Brainstorming is a quick way to fill slots in your plan. Jot down a target media outlet at the top of a piece of notebook paper. Quickly — in less than ten minutes — scribble one story idea per line until the pad is filled. Don't stop to criticize or censor yourself; just encourage the free flow of ideas. Odds are, you'll be able to go back and pick out a couple that sound worth doing.

When you're selecting ideas, remember not to pitch stories that are identical to past coverage. If a magazine just ran a piece on home security, perhaps quoting one of your competitors, it would be a waste of time to suggest a story about your views on the same subject. Instead, give the idea a new twist. How about a story on apartment security? Or vacation home security?

CUT THROUGH THE CLUTTER

Media outlets receive huge amounts of unsolicited publicity every day — in the mail, by fax, via e-mail, and over the phone. Because of this deluge, it is very difficult to get anyone to open your press release, much less get an editor to actually talk to you. Under these circumstances, busting through the clutter is an absolute requirement. Fortunately, as a guerrilla, it's also your prime directive. Here are a half-dozen paths to publicity prominence.

 Theresa Iglesias-Solomon started Niños, a bilingual education products catalog business, out of her home in Michigan several years ago. Realizing that her focus on the Hispanic market makes her newsworthy to economics editors looking to write about niche markets, she pursues the media constantly. She notifies them about new products and buying trends, all of which help to position her as an expert on the Hispanic market. Her efforts have resulted in articles in several prominent publications, including the *Wall Street Journal*, *Entrepreneur* magazine, *USA Today*, *Catalog Age*, and the Spanish-language publication *Vanidades*.

Be Topical.

Pick up a paper; watch a newscast. Is there any way you can hook yourself into what's happening? If there's a rash of burglaries, what a great chance to talk about your security service. If other travel agents are raising fees and yours are staying put, speak up.

When problems arose with Intel's Pentium chip, an alert guerrilla at Carnegie Mellon University won scads of exposure for the school by pitching a story to the national media about an obscure computer scientist who had developed a better way to test chips.

Make Something Happen.

There's an unwritten rule that a good job of covering news starts with two words: be there. It follows that if you can dream up an interesting enough event, a news organization will send somebody to report on it — just to make sure they don't get scooped by a competitor!

 TIP! Not every business needs coverage in *Time* or the *New York Times*. Do some research and target five solid media outlets to pursue. Send them releases every month for six months. Call the editor. Focus!

One way to obtain publicity is to approach various publications and offer to write articles for them about your area of expertise. Donna and Scott Lewein, who own the home-based Scribe Shop, have received most of their publicity as a result of the freelance writing they do. Scott recently sent an article on database publishing to *Entrepreneur* magazine. The editors turned down the article but asked him if, instead, he would be the subject of an article on home-based businesses.

Not just anything can be a news event. The days when reporters had enough time to attend a press conference are almost over. Unless you're Madonna, don't expect much of a turnout. But if you're stuffing people into Volkswagens, sponsoring a catfish-eating contest for charity, or putting the finishing touches on a luxurious new penthouse, you may have created a newsworthy event.

Even better, tie yourself into an already newsworthy event and make yourself the focus of the coverage. Alan Schulman did that when he made a big splash with his marine batteries at a national fishing trade show. He approached the show's organizers and asked them if he could run a contest during the show.

Alan's casting contest garnered a huge amount of publicity for him and his product because it made him one of the show's features. The newspapers that covered the show all talked about Alan, his contest, and his products.

Generate Data.

One of the best ways to create news is to assemble data that isn't readily available to the public. Pick a group of people to whom you have more access than most. Your customers would be a good place to start. Do a survey. Come up with a question or questions that tie into a current community issue.

Say you're in the home security business. Is crime up in your area? It would be interesting to know what percentage of people in town lock their doors at night compared to five years ago. Ask your customers, tabulate the results, and announce them to the local media. It may not work the first time, but the longer you do an annual, semiannual, or other regular survey, the more respectable, authoritative, and newsworthy you become.

Sandra Beckwith, the publisher of "The Do(o) Little Report," recently did a survey about cigar smoking. She sent a postcard to each of her readers asking two questions about men and cigars. Not only did she use the survey as a story for her newsletter, she was able to tabulate the results and send out a press release with her findings.

Sell Yourself as an Expert.

One manufacturer of burglar alarms monitors the media for reports of sensational crimes. When something suitable comes along, it faxes releases describing how the use of a particular safety product could have stopped or mitigated that crime.

Think of a similarly compelling topic of public interest, then organize and write up your thoughts into a pointed analysis. Be sure to arrive at some reasonably startling conclusions and include catchy items of advice or warning.

If you agree with the conventional wisdom, your comment isn't as appreciated and useful as the contrarian opinion. When the Gulf War was almost over, there were thousands of "experts" eager to talk about what a good idea the effort had been. But the few antiwar critics willing to be quoted were the ones that appeared in news stories.

Form a Group.

As a negotiation expert and president of a home-based software company in Brookline, Massachusetts, Dan Burnstein could be considered just another small businessperson. As president and co-founder of the Management Software Association, a group of expert-system software makers, he speaks for an entire industry. So what if it's a small industry. He still sounds like a big shot, and an unbiased one at that.

You don't have to sell expert systems to be considered an expert. All you have to do is get together with some of your colleagues, set yourselves up as a trade or professional group, and have yourself designated a spokesperson. This is an excellent opportunity for a guerrilla in a small but growing niche to achieve a national profile. You may be able to contact other prospective members through a larger umbrella group.

Terry Wohlers is a home-based consultant in Fort Collins, Colorado, as well as the chairman of the Rapid Prototyping Association (RPA), a thousand-person group affiliated with the Society of Manufacturing Engineers (SME). Terry was an expert on high-tech ways to rapidly build prototypes and models long before he founded the group two years ago. But now he is an official expert. The difference is huge.

Since forming RPA, Terry doesn't have to lift a finger to get publici-

TIP! Once you get publicity, put it to work. Copy press clippings or excerpt quotes and include them in every direct mail package you send out. There is no better way to gain instant credibility with your prospects.

ty. The publicity department at SME — which, by the way, pays all expenses for his group as well — churns out press releases featuring Terry's comments on the fast-growing industry. Reporters interested in rapid prototyping call SME and are referred directly to him. He's even met individually with the government's top technology officials in Washington, a feat he would never have been able to accomplish as a representative of a single home-based company. Since he became the spokesperson for a whole group of companies, Terry has so much business, he regularly turns down consulting and speaking gigs he once would have leaped at.

Present an Award.

Every year millions of us sit through lengthy awards ceremonies for the film, music, and television industries, not to mention the weeks of speculation in the media about who will win the next Emmy, Grammy, or Oscar. There is no way these industries could purchase the amount of exposure they get in exchange for a few pot metal trophies. You don't have to be in Hollywood to do the same.

If you run an industry-specific ad agency, have a contest to select the best ad in your niche. Make it an annual affair. You don't need cash or any prize beyond official recognition and perhaps a paper certificate. People will enter for the honor it confers on their company and for the publicity they can, in turn, generate for themselves if they win.

Alan Shulman, the home-based manufacturer of the Basement Watchdog, ran a contest among the retailers who carry his battery-operated sump pump for the best display. He announced the winner in a press release and used the story in his own promotional newsletter as well.

There are countless awards you could present on a local, national, specialized, or general-interest basis. If you're in the communications business, you could hold a contest to find the most talented writer among local high school students. If you're a financial consultant, hold an investing contest and certify the investor who gets the most paper profits over time as your town's "Top Stockpicker." If you run an interior decorating service, put together a panel to select the most beautiful living room in your community.

Be sure to notify appropriate media of the contest well before it starts, during its progress, and, of course, before the awards ceremony, which can be as splashy or as modest as you like. Either way, when you hand out that award, the winner won't be the only one who has gained something.

Give Something Away.

Henry David Thoreau once described doing good as "one of the professions that are full." Maybe that was true a century ago. Today someone who gives of time, money, or material to the needy is considered worthy of attention. For that reason, a little altruism should be part of every home-based guerrilla's marketing personality.

What should you give away? If there's a flood, a caterer could pour free coffee. If newspapers report that students are scoring below the norm on English tests, a copywriter could tutor them in composition. Let the media know about any community service you do, but be prepared to do it because it's the right thing to do, not because of the publicity. Otherwise you may find that the joy has gone out of the giving.

MAKING THE MOST OF IT

When your moment of fame arrives as the result of a successful publicity effort, don't let it vanish like yesterday's news. Be sure to wring the maximum worth out of it.

Copy those clips and use them over and over again. Include them in your direct mail pieces, in your sales kits, and in your media. (Note: Before reprinting an article, you may need permission. Check with your lawyer if in doubt.)

Dan Burnstein, who sells Negotiation Pro software through his home-based business, makes sure anything written about him lasts indefinitely. His press kit, mailed to all reporters inquiring about Negotiation Pro, includes a wide variety of clippings.

The oldest, from the *New York Times,* ca. 1991, is a computer column focusing on him and his product. That piece, sent out with new press releases, helped result in a 1992 piece in the *Wall Street Journal.*

More recently, Dan has been written up in publications as obscure as *Lawyer Hiring and Training Report* and as focused as *Training* magazine. Today, when reporters see Negotiation Pro's press kit, they are sure to respect the company for its longevity, influence, and authority.

When you get publicity, it's almost as if you hired a team of professional writers to find ways to describe your business. Concise, gripping statements that you might never have thought of on your own are like a bonus for your efforts. Donna Salyers, who sells faux furs out of an old Woolworth's building where she also has an apartment, had such luck when a copy editor stuck the headline "A Kinder, Gentler Fur Coat" on a story about her business. A slicker or catchier positioning statement is hard to imagine. Donna has used it in all of her marketing and advertising materials. Her business has been growing steadily ever since.

Be Prepared!

Many companies have been caught unprepared or with a low inventory after a favorable, influential report airs. When the public responds to the story, their service or product is not available.

Don't scoff. It happens! And the ill will built up when would-be customers' hopes are dashed can cripple or destroy a fledgling guerrilla enterprise.

Does that mean you should hire help, increase production, and open new locations as soon as you mail your first release? Not at all. But have a plan ready for when the good news hits. Be prepared to take names, send rainchecks, or do whatever it takes to deal with the demand.

PRESS RELEASE PRIMER: CREATING A PRESS PACKAGE

The basic tool of the guerrilla seeking publicity is a press release. This can be as simple as a single sheet of typing paper or as elaborate as a printed folder stuffed with brochures, color slides, and even audiovisual material. Its objective may be to inform someone you've never met about an upcoming event or to provide a knowledgeable reporter with detailed background about your business.

The media have come to expect a standard format; if you vary it, your material won't seem as professional. So the format of your press release is important — and easy to learn.

The headline of a press release is its positioning statement. In seven words or less, it tells the reader what's important. And given the volume of information most reporters face, the headline may be the only part of your press release that gets read.

Take the time to hone your headline. Try it out on a few peers. Don't be cute or funny. Be straight and interesting, and reporters will respond.

Put your company's name and the name of a contact person on the upper left of the first page, the date on the upper right. Center a headline describing your news about a third of the way down the page. Next, flush left, put the date that the material can be made public. In almost all cases, that date is today, but if you're alerting the press to something you don't want known for a while, you can postdate the release. Be sure to give everyone the same date or you'll burn bridges.

Envision the basic structure of a press release as an inverted pyramid.

Start with the most important, basic facts. Then progress to less critical details. This is probably the way the journalist will rewrite your story for publication. If you do it properly, many smaller outlets will use your release unchanged.

Start the body of the press release with a statement that sums up its entire contents. Every journalist learns to look for the five *W*s: who, what, where, when, why — and sometimes how.

Start with what a journalist will think is most important, not what you think is most important. That usually means avoiding quoting and naming yourself or your business in the first part of the first sentence. Say: "Valley residents bought burglar alarms in record numbers last month in response to the recent rise in crime, according to a local home security consultant." Don't say: "John Smith, the Valley's best security adviser, says Valley residents…"

The rest of the release should expand on the lead paragraph. For instance, in the second paragraph of the example above you might want to give the exact percentage increase in alarm purchases. In a later paragraph, break down how many were motion detectors, glass-break alarms, and so on.

Include a few quotes in your own words. The quotes should amplify a topic that was brought up in a prior section. Let's say one paragraph makes the point that citizens are buying alarms for protection. The next paragraph could be a quote saying that studies have shown that alarms are an effective deterrent to burglars.

To make sure the quote sounds natural, say it out loud. Avoid

> Kimberly Stanséll recently sent out a press release titled "Small Business Owners Publicly Confess Their Sins." The first paragraphs read: "Confession is good for the soul…and employees turned entrepreneurs candidly confessed their spendthrift habits that were costly to former employers. The confession forum: a recent workshop presentation of 'Six Ways to Stretch a Mini-Budget' at the National Home Office Expo in New York presented by Los Angeles-based Kimberly Stanséll, publisher of 'Bootstrappin' Entrepreneur: The Newsletter for Individuals with Great Ideas and a Little Bit of Cash.' Confessions included:" This first paragraph packed a punch! Not only did it provide some newsworthy information in the form of a survey, it also positioned Kimberly as an expert, introduced her newsletter, and gave the editor a reason to keep reading.

TIP! The most important part of your press release is the headline. It has to grab the editor's attention and position the release as newsworthy.

putting words in quotes that you would never use in conversation.

Make your press release distinctive by including a personal, possibly handwritten note introducing yourself and showing your knowledge of the reporter or editor you're addressing. Mention some of the person's past stories.

There's plenty of room for creativity here, especially for a guerrilla willing to risk being unconventional. Do something outrageous or at least unusual to draw attention. Delivering a press release attached to a helium balloon is something a professional PR firm probably wouldn't consider — which is just why it might work for you.

5 PRINTED MATERIALS
POSITIONING YOURSELF WITH PRINT

MOST GUERRILLAS WOULDN'T DREAM of meeting their largest customer or their banker dressed in dirty sweat pants. Yet they commit the same sort of marketing suicide when they send out a battered, poorly designed, poorly printed brochure or business card. Like advertising, your printed materials aren't an expense — they're an investment. Money invested now will pay big dividends later.

Pattianne Turner is similar to a lot of home-based guerrillas. She runs a desktop publishing business in Alvinston, Ontario, creating promotional materials, annual reports, and corporate publications for a variety of businesses. Nothing unique about that. So why is Pattianne thriving while many other desktop publishers are struggling? One reason is that she markets her services with low-cost, high-impact printed materials.

Her trifold brochure, printed on special paper and featuring her own design skills along with testimonials from grateful clients, is a powerful positioning tool as well as a detailed introduction to her business. Pattianne highlights her special services, like weekend hours and free consultations, and her absolute guarantee is prominently displayed.

Printed materials like Pattianne's brochure should be part of any guerrilla's marketing arsenal. They can be economical (just pennies each in some cases) without skimping. On the other hand, some businesses spend $10 or $20 for each brochure — an investment that can pay off on the first new job.

To keep her investment to a minimum, Pattianne used preprinted paper from a mail order catalog. She also designed and wrote the brochure herself. Of course, design is her business. A construction company shouldn't hesitate to call in a professional. It costs just as much to print an attractive brochure as an ugly one, and the attractive brochure will pay for itself much faster.

Other printed marketing materials include simple flyers, business cards, letterhead, invoices, order forms, and coupons. You can get significant marketing benefits from envelope stuffers, inserts, parts lists, price lists, and even gift certificates.

You never thought of these printed materials as marketing tools? You should. Any printed matter that is sent from your business is a marketing opportunity.

THE POWER OF PRINT

Give some serious thought to spending what may seem like a great deal of money on your printed materials. For many home-based businesses — especially those that deliver a service — the image and credibility gained from a substantial printed piece are well worth it.

Guerrillas know the power of a first impression. And the right materials can make it positive and lasting. After the sales call, when you've packed up your materials and gone home, your brochures remain, reminding the prospect of your terrific business.

Even if you can't afford the most expensive materials, you can still use guerrilla techniques to put together a brochure that will position your business and make an impact.

Don't stop with a handsome brochure. Anything you print will "talk" to your customers. Include a discount for special customers on your business card or a thank-you note on your invoice. Every invoice from Mike Lee's home-based printing prepress service goes out with a sales tagline printed on it and a thank-you. Like all guerrillas, he's selling at the same time he's collecting for past services.

Use your invoice to generate repeat customers and your letterhead, fax cover sheets, and business cards to position your company. That doesn't mean including a six-page essay with every invoice. But consider including a list of other services, a coupon toward a future purchase, or even a stack of referral cards customers can give to friends.

POSITIONING

Your printed materials have to be integrated with your positioning statement and with each other. If you want to be known as the fastest copywriter in the construction industry, make sure every message you send conveys that, from the language to the typeface.

Do your brochures look homemade? That's great for a home-baked pie company but probably not ideal for a tax lawyer. Is your business card heavier and better printed than your competitors'? That's a subtle way of implying that your product is of better quality as well.

BUSINESS CARDS

One of the most overlooked marketing tools is a simple, inexpensive square of paper. Astute guerrillas can take advantage of the American business card exchange ritual by using business cards to position themselves and reposition the competition. All in all, it's probably the most important printed material you'll create.

In most cases, you'll hand someone a business card while making a first impression. At that moment, you're a blank slate. Your card can make a huge difference in establishing your position. It's also a great way to spread the word about your business. You can afford to send dozens of cards to possible prospects or use in generating referrals.

Some businesses (like law) require fairly sedate cards. But you can add a specialty ("Specializing in tax planning for seniors") or even a credibility builder ("...since 1965"). And why not list your home phone number in addition to your office number to communicate your accessibility?

Don't forget the back of the card. It costs virtually nothing to print on the back, and there's so much you can say. If you want your card to be useful, memorable, and a "keeper," here's your chance.

Kimberly Stanséll uses a foldover business card that does double and even triple duty. She has enough information on the oversize folded card, including her positioning statement, to qualify it as a mini-brochure for her writing services. Customers say it gives them a definite feel for her capabilities. And she broke even on the extra expense for the

 TIP! Template software lets you create professional-looking flyers and brochures with very little effort. Don't worry about looking original. Looking good is more important.

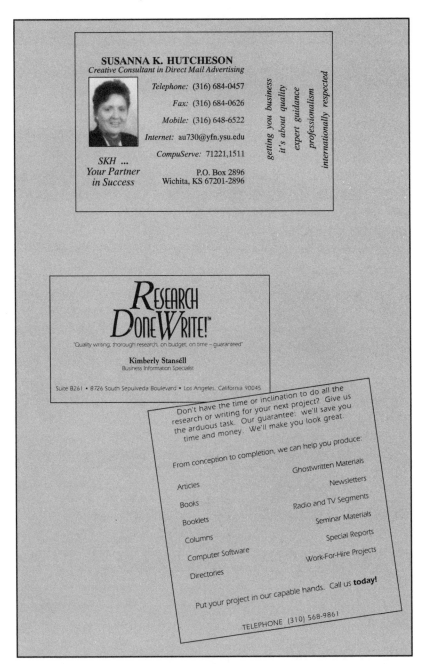

The business card at the top of the page is the six-panel infocard that home-based consultant Susanna K. Hutcheson uses. On the bottom is the cover and inside panel of Kimberly Stanséll's foldover card. Notice how much information she is able to convey on just her business card.

elaborate card by not printing costlier brochures.

Business cards don't have to break your marketing budget, but don't skimp! Use the best paper available and consider having your card professionally designed. An investment of a few hundred dollars in dynamite business cards is well worth the expense. And please think twice about using the laser-fed template business cards available from specialty paper stores. They rarely look as good because the perforations aren't finished and they often peel away, giving the card a very unprofessional look.

> Home-based marketing consultant Susanna K. Hutcheson gets a lot out of her business card. Rather than sending prospects a one-sided card with just her name and address, she hands out a business card–size brochure, or infocard, containing six panels of information. On the front of the card, she lists six different ways to contact her, including an internet address, CompuServe address, and mobile telephone number. That's accessibility!

What to Include.

Remember that the main goal of a business card is to make it easy to contact you. Your toll-free number, office number, home number, cellular number, fax number, and e-mail address all belong on your card. Giving out this information builds trust and relationships.

At the very least, it should include your name, the company's name, address, phone, and fax. Don't forget to tell people what business you're in and why you're in it. Kimberly's card positions her by including her service slogan: "Quality writing, thorough research, on budget, on time — guaranteed." You'd be amazed at how often people look at a business card that doesn't have a descriptive phrase with absolutely no recollection of who you are or what you do.

Once you cover the basics, you can dress up (and power up) your business card in any number of ways.

Here are some suggestions for getting more mileage out of your business card:

Are you a travel agent? Include useful information such as the 800 numbers of leading airlines, hotels, and car rental companies. People will stick your card in a purse or pocket and bless you when it comes in handy. If you are a real estate broker, a table for figuring mortgage payments on different amounts and interest rates would make your card invaluable for house hunters.

Is your home office in an out-of-the-way place? Print a small, readable map to your location on your card. If the drive is long, offer a 10%

discount as an incentive to anyone who presents your card when making a purchase.

Is your budget too tight for brochures? Use a bigger, folded card like Kimberly Stanséll's to convey a minibrochure's worth of information. Or try a mega-minibrochure called an infocard (page 68). This tiny cornucopia of information, up to eight panels long, will definitely make you stand out.

Do customers need your service infrequently? Try a card cut in the shape of a Rolodex insert. That way, customers will find it easier to file and find when they need it.

Having trouble getting a few key prospects to warm up? Use a standard, run-of-the-mill business card — but handwrite a note to grab their attention, show you understand their needs, and get them to save your card. An example: "Give (customer's name) a discount of 10% on any order when this card is presented."

Want clients to accept working with employees besides yourself? Print a profile of a key worker on your business card. Is there any better way to show that an employee will do the job just as well as you?

Having trouble describing your business in black and white? Business cards with full-color photographs are more expensive, but if you're a florist, artisan, photographer, or other visually oriented home-based guerrilla, a photo card will do far more than words alone.

If price is your marketing strength, you should display it on your card. Don't stop with a slogan, such as "Your Economy Tax Preparer." Print a full or abbreviated price list on the back. It won't take many extra sales to pay for itself.

Business cards are so inexpensive that you can afford to have several models printed to test which ones work best. Test your design, test whether you should include a discount or an informational tidbit, test the type of paper stock, and test the colors used in printing. Solicit feedback from your customers. Find out whether your card is an attention-getter, why it works or doesn't, and incorporate this response into your next set of cards.

Where and How to Distribute Your Cards.

As a general rule, you should hand out business cards wherever you can. But everybody already does that. Try putting your effort into finding

TIP! The two most important parts of any flyer are the headline and the order form. Make it easy for people to respond to you. If you post your flyer on a bulletin board, include your telephone number several times and in a way that people can tear it off and take it with them.

new and improved modes of distribution. You'll see a bigger payoff.

You can use your business card as a minibillboard. Many home-based businesses' entire marketing strategy consists of posting eye-catching business cards on bulletin boards in well-chosen public places. Supermarkets, apartment lobbies, Laundromats, college campuses, and community centers all draw certain kinds of people and often have bulletin boards.

One California real estate guerrilla hands an extra $3 and a business card to the toll collector as he crosses the bridge from exclusive Marin County into San Francisco. "I'd like to pay for the car behind me as well," he says. "Please give them this." Nine times out of ten, the other driver calls, at least to say thank you. He's sold several expensive homes as a result, and at 6% commission, he can afford to drive back and forth across the bridge all day, positioning himself in front of BMWs, Cadillacs, and Mercedes-Benzes.

Always give people more cards than they ask you for. As noted earlier, illustrator Stevie Ann Rinehart includes at least two business cards in every brochure she sends out. One is for the recipient, and the second is to be given to a friend or anyone else who might be interested in her work. It's an easy way to get referrals.

Of course, you ought to include a business card with every brochure, invoice, and letter as well. Even the phone bill gets opened by someone who might need insurance or whatever you offer.

LETTERHEAD

Most businesses only use 10% of the marketing potential of their printed letterhead. It doesn't have to be that way. Stationery can be a real marketing bargain, one that packs a wallop much greater than its cost.

From the day Theresa Iglesias-Solomon started her home-based catalog business, Niños, one glance at her stationery told you what business she was in. The fun-looking, full-color design of confetti with a fiesta flair clearly positions her business as one concerned with Hispanic culture and children.

It's appropriate for Theresa's letterhead to impart a fun-loving feel. Yours should mirror the image of your business. Remember, your stationery is a substitute for you. It should be dressed as you would for an important meeting, so use the best paper you can afford.

Theresa could have let the evocative design of her letterhead position her business all by itself. But why leave any doubt? Also include a positioning statement that states clearly what you offer and why people do business with you. Theresa's says "Bilingual Educational Products."

Why not go beyond brief positioning statements? Turn every sheet of letterhead into a minibrochure. List your full range of services. If your mail-receiving business also does typing, put it on your letterhead.

If your business changes, so should your stationery. We're not talking simply about a new phone number or address. Guerrilla Linda Abraham wants to expand the writing services she offers college students applying to graduate school. A new positioning statement on her letterhead will tell everyone that, in addition to writing personal statements, she can handle letters of recommendation, résumés, and other parts of the application.

Don't forget the envelope. If your business depends on getting prospects to open mail from you, do some research on what sort of envelope will get opened first. Try pastel colors, colored ink, or a phrase or positioning statement right on the envelope. One guerrilla has a black-and-white *New Yorker*–style cartoon printed on his envelope — a definite show-stopper.

Stationery starts with letterhead and envelopes, but it doesn't end there. Any piece of paper that passes through your hands (or, better, your customers' hands) during the course of a normal day can become a piece of guerrilla marketing letterhead.

Memo pads can be muscular marketers, especially if you or your customers go through a lot of them. Say you sell to an auto parts store where employees jot short notes all day long. Take a memo pad on your next visit — and leave it behind. It will hang around for days, weeks, or even months in high-traffic areas near the phone and cash register. Your name, logo, and address will be displayed to all comers.

Post-It notes are everywhere, and most of them sport nothing but handwritten scrawls. That's a shame from a marketing point of view. Why not put your logo there, and your phone number! Make sure you print them small enough so there's still room to write. Or try using a thin wash of ink so you can write over the print but still see your message.

Fax cover sheets are often overlooked as a marketing vehicle. Since they rarely require much in the way of a message, blow up your logo, expand your positioning statement, and add a complete list of your services and products.

Labels let you stick your marketing message on boxes, padded envelopes, computer disks, and any other container you send out.

Again, don't stop with your address. Include your logo and positioning statement as well.

You can even send your e-mail correspondence on "letterhead." Some online services let you design your own "signatures" and include them automatically at the end of your messages. Do so, by all means. Include everything you would on paper: address, phone, fax, positioning statement. Be careful about some e-mail signature conventions. Skip quotations in favor of your own positioning statement. (You don't want to risk offending people who disagree with a pithy saying.) Avoid overly fancy formatting that may get jumbled on a different service's software.

BROCHURES

Sending someone your brochure is an important part of the selling process, but it can't close a sale for you all by itself. As long as you recognize that, you can turn your brochure into a very powerful positioning tool that will introduce a prospect to your company and open the lines of communication, a crucial first step.

A brochure is a detailed description of your business, your products and services, and yourself. Larger than a one-page circular and shorter than a catalog, it's a versatile and effective resource that, when well designed and written, lets home-based guerrillas compete in the same arena with the big guys.

Doll designer Donna Hawley wants to give prospects a real feel for the vibrant colors and rich fabrics of her creations. Since she's in Nebraska and most of her customers aren't, a brochure is the best way she can provide that kind of product detail. Her four-color, high-quality brochure is not cheap to produce. But the combination of professional production, vivid imagery, and specific details are critical to showing off her product in the best light.

Three Main Concepts.

A brochure is an introduction, an icebreaker. It's an easy way to get a customer to take one small, unthreatening step toward you. Most small businesses don't spend enough on their brochures — and many big businesses spend too much.

Flashy, overproduced brochures don't always return their investment. Underproduced brochures never do. You do have to make sure yours is:

- Up to date.

- Complete.

- Focused.

Avoid dating your brochure. Say "In business since 1986" rather than "In business 10 years." Then you won't have to update your brochure every year.

Don't leave anything out of your brochure that will answer an important question or explain critical benefits, but don't offer information that might work against you, either. The more you tell the customer, the better, but don't ramble. Be concise and focused in the way you present yourself and your services. Use bulleted lists and boldface copy to set off the important points. Nobody will read your brochure if it is long and boring. Get to the point, and always take your audience into consideration.

Format.

The precise format depends on the message you want to convey. Modest brochures can be two sheets of paper folded in half and stapled into a pamphlet or booklet. That gives you eight pages. Each additional sheet adds four pages. (It also adds to the cost of paper, printing, and mailing.)

If your budget forces you to choose between skimping on design or production and making your brochure shorter, get out your blue pencil and start cutting. A good-looking, concisely written brochure is always stronger than a lengthy one that looks unprofessional.

Most brochures are printed on coated paper stock to improve the reproduction of illustrations. You can use plain white bond, however, if it fits your image and purposes. A consultant to nonprofit groups, for example, might do well to avoid a glossy, corporate look in favor of one that suggests frugality and prudence.

Brochures have been around forever. But there is always room for creativity. An odd size of paper, like 4 inches square (or 2 feet square) may be just the thing if your main goal is to say "I'm different!"

Content.

A brochure should start with a good headline. The positioning statement from your letterhead is probably a solid choice. If this seems too easy, remember: repetition is the guerrilla's secret weapon.

If you need to write a new headline, keep it short. Make sure it identifies your business. Make sure it positions you in the market. For example:

"A Win-Win Scenario ..."

"We are privileged to have access to services offered through CAST. Pattia Turner has been able to delight us a demanding customer."

Peter W. Angus, Presid
Foodservice Dynamics L

"Ms. Turner has provided invalua suggestions with respect to content organization of my business literature. Turner's work proves to be of exceptio quality and I would recommend her serv to anyone."

Maria Erdmann-Radd
Chartered Account

"Thank you so much for your support efforts in publishing our Annual Report. have had a great number of positive comme and we greatly appreciate your help."

Joyce Lambert, Executive Direc
The Canadian Red Cross Soci

"A major part of the success of our Gr Opening was due to CAST. Ms. Turn exceptional skills in the design of our me gift certificates and advertising provider with affordable quality work."

Dwayne Wilson, Ow
Cathedral Quarters Restaur

OTHER CLIENTS SERVED:

Cuddy International Corporation
McCormick Canada Inc.
Middlesex County Board of Education
St. Clair College of Applied Arts
Lambton College

**Linda Abraham
Writing & Editing**

Specializing in
Personal Statements

*For those who hate to write,
but must...*

Home-based computer consultant Pattianne Turner puts a panel of testimonials on the left on the back of her brochures. The brochure on the right was created by home-based writer Linda Abraham using preprinted desktop publishing paper.

- For a home handyman: Let George Do It!

- For a design firm: Concept & Design Solutions

- For a freelance editorial service: Accurate, Reliable, Compelling

Note that brochures should always list benefits, not features. A benefit is what the prospect receives for his money — he will make more money, feel better, live longer, look sexier. A feature, on the other hand, is what you offer — a half-inch drill press or a wide range of Nautilus machines.

Your brochure should name and talk about your products and services. Have friends unfamiliar with your business read your copy. If they can't clearly articulate your products' benefits, you need to go back to the drawing board.

Include testimonials from satisfied customers. Use their photos or company logos if you can. Use long testimonials from several different types of customers. If a prospect sees a glowing detailed recommendation from someone that sounds like himself (or, even better, someone he actually knows), your chances of gaining a customer go up dramatically.

By all means, include photos or illustrations. The combination of good paper stock, professional printing, and skilled photography can yield a dynamite brochure at a reasonable cost. Definitely consider using photos or illustrations if you:

- Sell a product or service that derives most of its value from appearance. Examples include home renovators, antiques dealers, artisans, painters, graphic designers, and lawn care services.

- Have a complex concept that needs a graphic explanation. Perhaps you are selling a home water filtration system that uses new technology. A simple illustration may show customers how it works much faster and more thoroughly than words.

- Rely on your personal image to connect with customers and prospects. This can be very helpful if you are, for instance, a real estate agent who has worked for several different companies. Rule of thumb: If your face is more familiar to customers and prospects than your company name, put your face in the brochure.

But be warned. The two mistakes home-based businesses make with

TIP! Let your position in the marketplace help you decide how to create your printed materials. If you own a homespun crafts business, your printed materials should reflect a personal touch and homemade look. If, however, you are an accountant catering to Fortune 500 executives, the homespun look won't cut it.

their brochures have to do with photography. Mistake #1: Not enough photos. Mistake #2: Lousy photography, poorly reproduced. Get a professional to do it, or don't do it at all.

Distribution.

Hank Walshak, a home-based public relations executive in Pennsylvania, gave us these pearls of wisdom: "Just having a fancy four-color brochure means nothing if all you do is mass-mail it to unqualified prospects. A brochure is a great thing to send someone you may already have talked to or targeted as being interested in what you have to say."

You should never rely on a brochure to build a relationship with a prospect. Do your homework first. Find a list of people who you think would be interested in your services. Don't mail an unsolicited brochure. Most likely, it will end up at the bottom of the pile on a desk, or worse yet, in the trash.

Throughout the rest of this book, we talk about techniques you can use to generate leads and qualify prospects, including classified ads, direct mailings, telephone calls, newsletters, and inexpensive flyers. One way to follow up with these prospects is with your brochure.

Following up on direct responses is more cost-effective than sending unsolicited mail. It allows home-based guerrillas to focus their resources on the hottest prospects. This is a classic one-two guerrilla marketing punch. Many home-based businesses have survived and prospered using very little else.

Home-based Boulder management consultant Antonio Nuñez consults to Fortune 1000 CEOs. He never mails his brochures cold. Instead, he gets a personal referral from a peer. A cover letter prominently mentions this other CEO. The prospect then looks at Antonio's brochure in a more receptive frame of mind. The brochure–personal letter combo is time-tested and effective.

It bears repeating that the purpose of a brochure is not to close the sale. It's used to introduce yourself, inform prospects of your capabilities, educate them about new concepts, and help you get the appointment to close the sale — later.

A brochure is one part of building a relationship. You should *never* rely on it to build or even start a new relationship for you on its own. So do the research, find the target, and then follow up in many ways, perhaps with a brochure.

 Guerrilla home-based business planner Marcia Layton uses her fax cover sheet as a marketing tool. Receive a fax from Marcia and listed on the cover is her positioning statement and a detailed list of her services. It has opened the door for more work from several of her existing clients by reminding them of other services she can provide.

FLYERS

A flyer (also called a circular) is a single sheet of paper printed on one or both sides. It's less informative than a brochure and less costly. For the right job, however, it can be just as effective.

Chris Beal, the secondhand computer marketer, generates calls to his 800 number by posting flyers on university campuses all over the country. How can a home-based business afford that? Chris uses a posting service that, at minimal cost, distributes his flyer nationwide. Though inexpensive, his flyer is far from slipshod. Like his classified ads, it has a carefully crafted low-key look, which Chris has found very effective.

The goal of designing and producing a flyer is to keep the cost down to a few pennies per copy. That's because you want to distribute it literally (and liberally) anywhere a prospect might be:

- Slip them under automobile windshield wipers.

- Tape or tie them to utility poles.

- Thumbtack them to bulletin boards.

- Hand them out on city sidewalks or at suburban malls.

- Pile them in office lobbies or supermarket flyer racks.

- Fold them into self-mailers and send.

- Enclose them with direct mail pieces, invoices, and other mail.

A flyer is not as detailed as a brochure, so descriptions should be briefer. Use more lists and bullets for quick reading and saving space. You can still hit most of the same major points. Include:

- A headline (that may double as a positioning statement).

- A positioning statement if it's not in the headline.

- An illustration or photo.

- A little about your company, to create a personal tie.

- Names and descriptions of your products and services.

- Major features.

- Benefits to users (this is critical).

- Brief testimonials or a list of recognizable customers.

- A map to your location if you are hard to find.

- Hours of operation (stress if they're unusual or beneficial).

- Details about how to contact you by phone, on foot, and by mail.

- A request for action in the form of a visit, call, or letter.

About the only thing you can't do with a flyer is count on it to close sales. A flyer, even more than a brochure, is an introduction, an ice-breaker and first step. Use it to generate leads, follow up on leads, and prepare people for your call.

INVOICES AND ORDER FORMS

An invoice can do a lot more than end a transaction. Why not have it start a new one? You can do the same with order forms. If someone is ordering now, smooth the way for them to order again. A simple "Thank you" on an invoice or a reminder to "Order soon for Christmas delivery" on an order form can keep sales flowing. And, like all your printed materials, these forms should contain your phone numbers, location, hours of operation, credit terms, and position statement.

But before you get carried away with using these forms to hand out information, remember that they need to be functional. Make them easy to use. A well-designed order form can be a pleasure to fill out. A complex one, with tiny boxes and tinier type, may kill the sale.

You can use your business forms to generate repeat buying by devoting part of them to coupons, special offers, and even gift certificates. Frequent-buyer points, collected by clipping a corner from every invoice, is a novel way to build repeat business.

CUTTING THROUGH THE CLUTTER

Even the most mundane pieces of business information can contain a marketing spin. Product information sheets can list specifications in a dry, engineer's style, but it's far more effective to have them reflect your

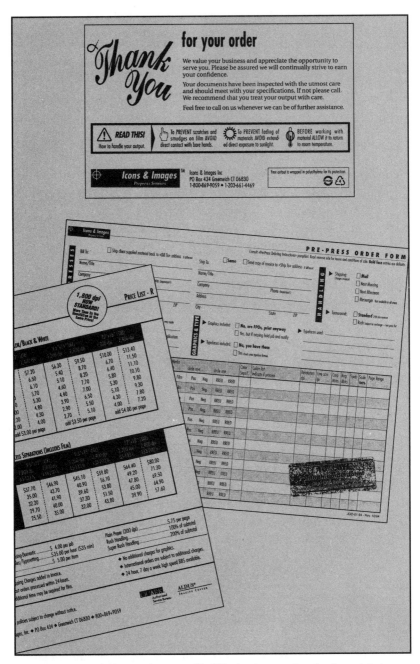

Home-based preprinting services guerrilla Mike Lee is a master at using printed materials to communicate with his customers. He includes the thank-you postcard at the top of the page with every order he sends out. Even his price list and order form are marketing tools. Notice the stickers he puts on each one.

individual approach to the business.

The weekly flyer from wholesaler the Stereo Advantage is filled with caricatures of each phone salesperson, along with a running commentary on which products offer superior performance. It's more fun to read than the competition's and, judging from its incredible success, more effective as well.

A positioning statement and contact information won't detract from the hard facts on a product data sheet and can lead to sales. While you're at it, a paragraph explaining why your product has these features (benefits to customers, of course) would not be amiss.

Use your price list to hit the decision-maker with a few factors besides the cost of a purchase. There is no better time to remind a customer that you have extended service warranties, weekend hours, free parking, and are committed to the highest quality.

Envelope stuffers are smaller than flyers and therefore contain less information. They're designed to fit regular envelopes with letters, invoices, statements, order forms, and any other communication. An envelope stuffer lets you raise the marketing wattage without raising your postage bill.

Home-based illustrator Robert Pizzo pays a little extra for reprints of an ad he runs in an annual design directory. The reprints go into every piece he mails out, increasing his impact at virtually no cost.

Be consistent in your materials. Repeat yourself a lot. And make sure your materials are sophisticated and well produced.

WHO CREATES YOUR PRINTED MATERIALS?

Having an outside expert do either the design or writing or both will increase the cost of your printed materials. But this added expense is an investment. If you're in an industry where appearance counts, skimping on your printed materials will cost you in the long run.

At the very least, rely on the best designer you can find to create a look for your company. Have her do the first iteration of your brochure, letterhead, business cards, and invoices. Then you'll have a template you can use forever. As you create new materials, you can hire an art student to knock them out for you based on the existing standard.

If your budget is tight and your print runs are small, you won't be able to afford a completely custom approach. That's where the wonderful new preprinted papers come in.

Several mail order companies sell preprinted forms, papers, and cards that can be used at your printer's or even on your laser printer. They do the expensive four-color printing on exotic paper, and all you have to do is add the text and black-and-white illustrations. The paper itself is fairly expensive, but it's cheap compared with the cost of printing that sort of effect yourself.

Most of the companies also offer template software that makes it easy to lay out the text so it will fit perfectly on the preprinted papers. To get started, call Paper Direct at (800) 272-7377, Queblo at (800) 523-9080, or Beaver Prints at (800) 847-7237. They'll send you a catalog along with a sheaf of hundreds of sample pages (for a small charge).

Take the samples to your designer and find a set that works. Using the template, the designer ought to be able to create a terrific look for you for very little. Then you can create the brochures and letterhead as you need them. If your prices change, there's no problem. Just type in the new data and run some more.

In our experience, the subtle papers work better than the more flashy designs. The prospect will read your letter instead of gazing at the paper. And avoid the business cards that you print yourself. The old-fashioned ones cost almost as little and look better.

Robert Pizzo's envelope-size direct mail pieces. Robert designed them so he could stuff them into all of his outgoing mail. See page 81.

6 DIRECT MAIL
LEVELING THE GUERRILLA PLAYING FIELD

IF THE FOUNDATION OF GUERRILLA MARKETING is creating a one-to-one relationship with prospects, what's the single most cost-effective way to accomplish this? A stamp. Your federal government gives you unlimited access to anyone in the country for 32¢.

Direct mail works. You can put your message right on your target's desk. You can reach anyone — from homemakers to executives to legislators. If you're good, you can grab their attention and hold it until they become customers.

Direct mail is the great equalizer. No person no matter how wealthy, no corporation no matter how large, has any better chance of having a letter opened than you do (with the possible exception of the IRS).

GUERRILLA DIRECT MAIL VS. REGULAR DIRECT MAIL

Guerrilla direct mail and regular direct mail are not the same thing. In fact, they are fundamentally different. Ordinary direct mail is a lot like panning for gold. The goal of the ordinary direct mail campaign is to sift through as much silt as possible, hoping for the occasional gold nugget. Of course, the home-based guerrilla marketer can't afford to send out a hundred letters for every hot lead. That hit rate might soon lead to bankruptcy.

The big catalog company that stuffs your mailbox every other week lives or dies by how tightly expenses on that mailing have been controlled. A few pennies per catalog either way can make the difference between record profits and dangerous losses.

Several years ago, guerrilla Bob Westenberg ran an advertiser-driven card deck mailing out of his home. He used direct mail to keep up with his advertisers. He sent them "Thank-U-Grams" annually to thank them for their business. He sent notes to prompt payers telling them how important it is to the "little guy" to get payment on time. Every time a yearly advertiser renewed an account, Bob would send the client a dinner chit with a note stating that although he couldn't fly out to provide dinner in person, he wanted to do so "by proxy." One advertiser even sent back a photo of himself and his wife having dinner "on Bob."

Guerrilla direct mail takes a different tack. Instead of trying to reach the maximum audience, it focuses on generating the highest hit rate. How high? Macintosh computer reseller Christian Beal gets responses from up to 75% of the mail he sends. A big mailer would smile at 1%, beam at 1.5%, and throw a party at 2%.

Take advantage of your size when fighting for business in the mailbox. Remember that you need to add only a few customers to turn a lousy year into a profitable one. General Motors, on the other hand, would go under fast if it increased its sales by only one, five, or even fifty cars a year.

There are only 800 names on the mailing list that guerrilla Ilise Benun uses to promote her marketing and self-promotion consulting practice. But they are highly targeted names. Ilise mails to them quarterly, often suggesting special consulting projects or announcing her latest workbook. A large direct mailer wouldn't find it worthwhile to mail anything to just 800 names, much less with an offer to sell one or two products or services.

Giant marketers have to focus on market segments. You can focus on individuals. Because you're small, you can pick fifty people who will make a difference to your business. You will learn their habits, understand their needs, and deliver a product or service that addresses those needs.

Doll designer Donna Hawley understands the importance of dealing with people as individuals even through the impersonal medium of direct mail. She doesn't rely solely on computer-generated mailing lists. She asks current customers for the names of people who might like to receive one of her brochures. She then includes a second brochure, specifically asking the recipient to pass it on to a friend.

NINE SECRETS OF DIRECT MAIL

Direct mail is a science. Every mailing can be tested, although the results aren't always intuitive. Direct mail marketers spend a great deal of time and money determining what works and what doesn't.

Testing doesn't make sense for only the big guys. It is the core of guerrilla marketing. Here are nine direct mail secrets, all of which are worth testing on your audience.

- Get their attention.

- Be conversational.

- Don't be brief.

- Make it easy to say yes.

- Start the relationship; don't close the sale.

- Follow up.

- Target, target, target.

- Get a name.

- Do your homework.

Get Their Attention.

A letter that isn't opened isn't worth much to you. To avoid such a fate, take a look at the direct mail pieces you are getting from big mailers. Whatever they're doing, do something different. If they use laser-printed addresses, write yours by hand. If they use postage meters or prepaid bulk mail postage, slap on stamps you licked yourself.

Why? Because the language of corporate direct mail — lots of "junk," most of it not relevant to the recipient — is the wrong language for you. If people believe you're sending them junk mail, your hit rate goes way down. Use regular stamps, overnight mail, unique packaging, or an imprint on the envelope to get your prospect's attention.

John Langdon is a self-taught, home-based designer and lettering artist who has been freelancing for over seventeen years. When he mails out information on his services, prospects rip open the envelope, even when it's unsolicited.

 Dress up your envelope. If it looks hand- rather than mass-mailed, it's more likely to get opened. Use a variety of colorful, even out-of-date stamps and try addressing each envelope by hand.

Why? First, Langdon's envelope is addressed by hand. It has colorful, totally unrelated stickers all over it. Anyone who sees it wonders what it contains. True-guerrilla Langdon considers the envelope — along with everything else he does — as an opportunity to get noticed. He considers it his obligation not to do anything ordinary, and that includes an ordinary envelope.

Of course, if your business is more serious, you don't want to send a frivolous envelope. A funeral home, for example, could probably get letters opened by plastering a cartoon on the outside, but it wouldn't translate into a higher response rate.

You have several tools at your disposal:

- Stamps. Most philately stores (which sell to stamp collectors) have a stock of thirty- or forty-year-old stamps that they'll be happy to sell you at close to face value. These stamps are still valid, and they make a creative, intriguing message on your envelope. Use three or four stamps on each envelope, making it really clear that the letter is indeed personal.

- The way you address the envelope. Perhaps the worst word to use is "Occupant." If you don't know the name of your prospect, you're probably better off not mailing the letter at all. Once you do have the proper name (be sure you spell it correctly!), either write the envelope by hand, type it, or use a laser printer that can print directly on envelopes.

- A tag line on the envelope. While personal letters never include this, it might be helpful in direct mail. One accountant sent out letters with "Open Immediately. Important Tax Information Enclosed" emblazoned on the front.

Be Conversational.

The typical direct mail letter is about as warm as a block of ice. Warm yours — and your prospects' hearts — by talking to them directly as if you were already friends. Don't adopt the traditional "sell" voice.

Christian Beal is the home-based guerrilla who sells refurbished Macintosh computers. His primary market is the college student population, a group that tends to be suspicious of corporate America and any communication that sounds like Big Business. Chris deals with that hur-

 TIP! Try using a postcard instead of a letter. You save the cost of the envelope and lower the postage. Most important, you don't have to convince anyone to open an envelope.

dle with a direct mail voice as unpretentious as a keg party.

One week after he sells a computer, he sends the customer a letter: "Because word of mouth is the most effective form of advertising available, we're willing to bribe you for it. Here's the deal. On the back of this letter you will find space for the names and addresses of five people you know who are potentially in the market for a refurbished Macintosh computer. Complete the form and return it in the enclosed envelope and we'll send you a copy of the shareware program SoundMaster (for free). Once we receive your list, we'll send our information to your referrals. If one of them buys a computer system from us, we'll send you a check for $25."

Twenty-five dollars is not much compared to the price of a new computer, and the shareware Chris distributes is available to anyone for no charge at all. But an unheard-of 75% of his customers return the referral sheet. His pitch works so well because he puts it in a conversational, one-to-one voice that his target market will listen to.

So what's the secret of writing a conversational letter? Don't write it at all. Instead, dictate it into a tape recorder, preferably while looking into a mirror. Then transcribe the tape, edit it, and you're in business.

P.S. Always, *always* add a postscript. First, because it's natural in a personal note. Second, because research shows that this is the most read part of any letter. You read this paragraph, didn't you?

Don't Be Brief.

If your prospects are interested in what you're proposing, they'll be willing to read a lot about it. If not, they'll never get past the first few lines. So assume you're writing to people who want to hear what you have to say, and say all of it.

Here's an analogy: If you went to make a personal sales call, how long would you talk for? Would you leave the prospect's office before she asked you to? Of course not. Treat your letter the same way.

When they get to the end of your letter, they'll have made a commitment of time, at least. A skillful guerrilla turns that time commitment into a solid business relationship.

Don't take our word for it. Test it. Send long letters and short letters, and see which works better.

The most tested, most proven, least intuitive message about direct mail is the longer, the better. No exceptions.

This scares some people. They worry about boring the reader or that they won't have enough to say. They hesitate to send a three- or five-page letter to a total stranger.

The World's Smallest Newsletter
Published on the 17th by:
BOB WESTENBERG
Copywriter / Consultant / Fund Raiser
95 Devil's Kitchen Dr. • Sedona, AZ 86351 • (602) 284-1111
FAX: (602) 284-2390

12 / 4

Classified ad: "Professional mixing bowl set perfect for serious cook with round bottom for efficient beating."

Most popular participatory U.S. sports: Swimming, exercise, walking, bike riding. Most popular spectator sports: Horse racing, pro baseball, college football.

Americans spent 70 times as much on gambling in '93 as they did on movies.

Paint company booklet says babies cry more and adults find it tiring when surrounded by the color yellow.

Octavio Guillen and Adriana Martinez of Mexico were engaged for *67 years.*

Average American spends 49 hours in a lifetime seeing doctors...and 64 hours waiting to see them.

Foreign visitors to the U.S. have trouble counting their change because our coins have no numerical markings.

Eat something healthy and filling before going to a party or other tempting situation if you're on a diet. You'll eat less if you do.

"Psycho" had the only movie musical score using only strings. It cost $800,000 to make and earned $16 million.

If you send a card to someone in the hospital, put their return home address on envelope. If they've left, card will be forwarded to them, not sent to you.

Walt Disney was once fired by a newspaper. The reason? Lack of ideas!

Most visible car color: White. It's seen 12 times more quickly than a black one. Red is difficult to see at twilight or in fog, as are all dark colors.

While TV watching, average viewer changes channels 325,393 times in his life.

It's getting harder to win product liability lawsuits. Only 41% of plaintiffs win today vs. 54% in 1987.

If all the chickens KFC cooked last year were laid beak to claw, they'd reach 23,580 miles *past the moon.*

Average exec wastes 45 minutes a day looking for misplaced information.

Many 18th century sailors had a crucifix tatooed on their backs hoping to deter ship captains from lashing them.

No "commercial" here this issue.. just all good wishes from Jeanne and me to you for a stress-free, happy holiday and a new year with all you hope for, and more.

Bob Westenberg's newsletter/postcard mailing. See page 95.

First and foremost, discuss the reader's needs. Demonstrate your understanding of your prospect's problems. From his Connecticut home, Wayne Clarke runs several businesses, including one as a representative for a multilevel distribution company. When he is writing to a prospect, he goes on for several pages. He spends much of it not on himself or his product but on the prospect's needs. He knows that people want extra income and the ability to work from home. So he makes sure they know he knows.

Be sure to show similar knowledge and understanding of your prospect. Wayne does that by mentioning the prospect's spouse, children, job, and other individual details. These items make the reader feel that Wayne knows him or her personally. They help to build a personal tie between the guerrilla and the potential customer.

Make It Easy to Say "Yes."

Okay. You've chosen the right list. Got the envelope opened. Impressed the prospect by understanding her needs. Now what?

Too often, mailers forget to make it easy. The prospect isn't going to spend a lot of time trying to figure out what to do next.

Do you want a phone call? If so, you may want to use a toll-free 800 number (unless you're trying to stress how local you are). Once you've got a phone number, flaunt it. Mention it on every page of the letter in bold type.

If you'd rather have a response by mail, make that easy as well. Include a self-addressed envelope — already stamped if you want to make an impact. Need them to fill in some information? You already know their name and address, so don't make them fill it in for you — do it for them.

Don't forget about timing. The temptation is to put direct mail aside, to say "I'll do it later." Give a prospect a bonus or a special gift for answering promptly. Maybe the first hundred callers get something for free or a special discount.

Test your response mechanism. Discover what works best and stick with it.

Start the Relationship; Don't Close the Sale.

It's hard to get a complete stranger to sit down, write a check, address an envelope, fill out an order form, and send it to you on the basis of a letter. So don't ask your prospects to do that right off the bat. Instead, ask

TIP! Make a big deal of your guarantee. Don't hide it. Set it off in a box.

In her book *Homemade Money*, Barbara Brabec stresses the need to follow up on any direct mail campaign. When a customer inquires about her books and newsletters, Barbara mails them her catalog, knowing that she isn't likely to get an order right away. If she follows up with a postcard or newsletter two to three months later, her response rate goes up to 4% or more.

for permission to send a free sample or continue with a phone call.

Once you've decided that you aren't going to sell a product, figure out what you want to do. If your goal is to set up a meeting, make that clear. Mention it several times. Don't hide the reason for your letter.

Donna and Scott Lewein run the Scribe Shop from their Wisconsin home. They've developed a series of stuffers, direct mail pieces that fit in a standard No. 10 envelope. They create new stuffers all the time and include them in every piece of mail that leaves the office. But the stuffers aren't sales pitches. They are marketing tools that try to get prospects to accept the Leweins as helpful, knowledgeable experts in their field. They have had stuffers on plain paper typesetting, competitive advantage tips, database publishing, and even an announcement of their one-year anniversary. Donna Lewein calls the stuffers low-key marketing pieces.

High-impact home-based guerrilla marketing is built on using such apparently low-key marketing tools to focus on individuals and build personal relationships.

Follow Up.

The best way to lose money is to send mail and wait for the phone to ring. Make it easy for your prospects — follow up.

Don't give up. The first letter doesn't always work. One contact every week for three months often does. Mike Lee, the owner of Icons & Images, is tenacious in keeping up a constant, gentle presence in his customers' and prospects' minds.

Mike takes advantage of every opportunity to put his message before his target audience. He treats all outgoing mail as if they were direct mail marketing pieces — which, of course, they are.

He sends occasional direct mail letters and more frequent postcards to clients and candidates. He regularly includes savings coupons, his own professional-looking brochures, and tips on making the most of printing relationships. This variety gives him a lot of excuses for contacting his targets, and it gives them a lot of reasons to pay attention.

Even his invoices carry a sales tag and a thank-you for buying from him.

Your followup doesn't have to be by mail. One successful guerrilla put a dollar bill in every letter he sent out. When following up by phone, he always managed to get past the secretary by saying, "I'm following up on the letter I sent last week — there was a dollar bill inside."

It's not advisable to continue mailing forever to someone who shows absolutely no interest in your message. But if you carefully select the fifty or a hundred people who are most likely to buy from you, you are well positioned to be more persistent than any conventional marketer could justify.

Linda Abraham writes and edits personal statements for UCLA students to include in their graduate school applications. This narrow market is perfect for direct mail.

 Tonia Davis gets our vote for the youngest guerrilla marketer of the year. At the age of 10 (with a bit of help from her mom and her 11-year-old brother), she started a baking company from her home in Castine, Maine. Tonia handled the marketing for Davis Baking Co. She had used highly targeted direct mail to gross almost $30,000 by her third summer in business. Her most effective campaign involved acquiring the mailing list of a nearby summer camp. She mailed brochures to the campers' parents, offering to deliver homemade cookies to their kids.

Linda wisely starts her marketing with mailing lists built from students who attend her lectures on writing and editing. She follows the lecture with a letter offering to help them with their personal statements.

But it takes a second, shorter letter, which she calls a reminder, to bump her response rate up from 5% to 8%. That's phenomenal by most direct mail standards. But it's well within the grasp of any guerrilla who follows up conscientiously, imaginatively, and persistently.

Target, Target, Target.

Direct mail experts rarely agree, but they are unanimous about one thing: The list you choose is the most important element of your mailing. It's more important than the offer, and far more important than the execution. Choosing the right list, finding the targeted hotbed of consumers itching to buy your product, is the secret of doing well with direct mail.

One of the biggest mistakes you could make as a home-based guer-

TIP! When people receive mail, they usually read the salutation first and the P.S. next. So your P.S. should contain your most attractive benefit, your invitation to action, or anything that inspires an urgent feeling. Try handwriting your P.S. Even better — make it personal.

rilla would be to buy into the "more is always better" philosophy. Publishers Clearinghouse, one of the largest direct mail marketers, lives and dies by it. It blankets the country with mail in the hope that a very small percentage of people will respond. You will only die by it. Leverage your strengths by selecting a handful of companies that could buy, and buy a lot, of what you're selling. You'll mail far fewer pieces and get many times the response rate of ordinary direct mail by focusing on a handful of individuals or companies. Forget the rest.

Doll designer Donna Hawley isn't afraid to look beyond her home of Nebraska for customers. But when she uses direct mail, she makes sure she's sending only to those most likely to be interested in what she has to offer.

For one campaign, Donna started with a list of guilds that manufacture dolls. She researched the guilds carefully, decided on the best way to reach them, and pursued with a mailing and follow-up phone calls.

Get a Name.

Never mail to a company name or street address alone. Mail to Resident or Purchasing Agent may as well be marked Trash. The guerrilla's whole advantage in marketing lies in the ability to create and pursue personal relationships. To do that, you have to at least know someone's name.

There are any number of ways to get a name. If you know nothing more than the company's name, look up articles about the firm in trade journals, where executives' names and even pictures and biographies often appear.

You can call the company president's office. Ask a secretary whom you should contact about office supplies, meeting planning services, or whatever you are marketing.

Go to trade shows and conferences to find the real heavy hitters. You'll get unparalleled access to people who make decisions. But don't try to sell them anything during these high-intensity exchanges. Instead, give them a business card and then follow up with a personal letter.

The more details you have about the person behind the name, the better. Donna Hawley does not rent a general retailers' list with thousands of anonymous names. Instead, she asks customers to tell her about shops they know that carry similar merchandise. If necessary, she phones to get a person's name. Then she can write to them armed with knowledge no list can offer. Personal, focused, persistent — that's the essence

TIP! Don't stop mailing to a list until the results can't justify the expense. Many people don't respond until the third or fourth letter.

of the home-based guerrilla's marketing strategy.

Do Your Homework.

A guerrilla direct mail marketing campaign doesn't start at the post office or even your typewriter or computer. Start at the library, at a newsstand, a bookstore, or perhaps your target company's headquarters.

Bob Westenberg, a home-based copywriter and consultant, gets most of his business by mailing out a monthly postcard he calls "IMP: The World's Smallest Newsletter." He fills each card with interesting news tidbits, and at the end of the card he puts in a small plug for himself. Last year, the mailing produced $21,000 worth of work for Bob.

If it's a public company, read its annual report. Call any public company's investor relations office for a free annual report. These documents contain everything from last quarter's interest expenditures to the chairman's predictions of the most exciting upcoming developments.

To a guerrilla mailer, an annual report is a source of precise addresses, names, and titles. It may describe new product lines, budgets for certain items, or photographs of officers and facilities. Careful study of this marketing gold mine can make you seem like an insider even if you've never heard of the company before.

Trade magazines are another good source for names and information. Someone who has been promoted or hired is probably looking for new vendors to work with — a perfect opportunity for you. Attaching an article that mentions the person favorably is a great way to break the ice.

Privately held companies also have information you can get easily. Nothing will tell you more about their business than their own product catalogs. You'll find out what they're selling, how they're selling it, to whom they're selling, their price points, service and warranty policy, shipping methods, and more. And you can get all this inside information, in many cases, with no more than a toll-free telephone call.

When guerrilla writer, consultant, and seminar leader Marcia Yudkin quit college teaching to become a writer, her first assignment came from the *New York Times*. She landed the prestigious credit by using guerrilla direct mail.

When Marcia discovered that the *Times* was starting a new education section, she found out the name of the editor of the section and pitched him an article. She wrote a personal letter, highlighted her background,

TIP! When writing a direct mail letter, let people know within the first eight or ten lines what you are selling.

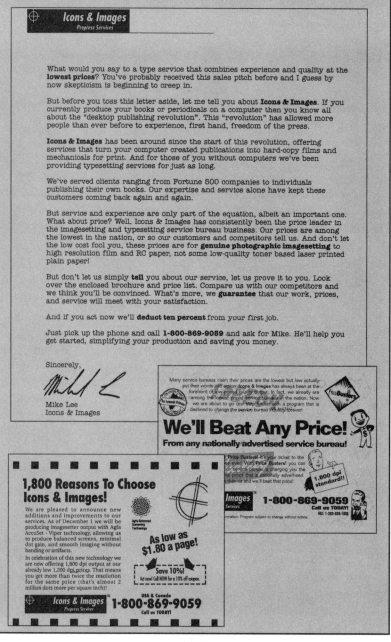

A direct mail letter and two postcards sent out by home-based typesetter Mike Lee. All three pieces stress Mike's guarantee and call the recipient to respond by offering a discount.

Christian Beal, the home-based refurbished Macintosh seller, mailed this postcard to over 3,500 customers on his mailing list. Three days later the phone started ringing. It didn't stop until December 31. Final result: $27,000 in sales.

demonstrated her skills, and asked for a chance to show what she could do. Perfectly targeted, timed, and focused, her proposal won her the kind of credibility that can make a guerrilla's career.

ANATOMY OF A GUERRILLA DIRECT MAIL LETTER

Once you've got the name, the offer, and the envelope, everything comes down to the letter. It should be personal, sometimes even written by hand. Yes, a computer-generated letter would be faster, neater, and look more high-tech. But when appropriate, nothing makes a more personal statement than a handwritten letter. If you opt to type or print out your letter, at least attach a note with a comment in your own writing.

In the letter, aim for a style that stands out from the formal, all-business tone of many direct mail solicitations. A recent magazine subscription offer started: "Dear Mr. Smith: I believe you'll find it interesting to read about the richest men and women in America. That's why I'm inviting you to send for a copy of..." Stiff? Formal? You bet. It's the exact opposite of a guerrilla's approach.

Here are specific tips on how to make your letter successful.

- Date. Big mailers may be preparing mailings that won't go out for months. For you, it should be as simple as a glance at the calendar. Put today's date.

- Name. Never include just a title. Call to make sure of the spelling unless you're absolutely sure. Think you can slide by? What do you do with direct mail that misspells your name?

- Title and address. Again, have everything correct. Phone to check if you have any doubt. You might be forgiven for calling someone by the wrong title, especially if she's recently been promoted. But won't it help your cause if you seem to know about her new job before the ink is dry on the new stationery?

- Dear "first name." Should you use a first name or honorific like Mr. or Ms.? In these informal days, you're usually better off with a first name unless the person you're addressing is unusually stuffy. As a rule of thumb, use the name you would use if you were speaking to her in person.

 TIP! Always test your direct mail letters. Hunches and intuition don't count in this sort of marketing.

- First paragraph. Always include a reference and a benefit. Mention who referred you or how you found the prospect. Explain how what you're offering will help her. A letter without a referral is hardly worth the stamp. Even if the referral is just a mention of a newspaper article, it is better than nothing.

- Proof and details. What's your customers' biggest worry? How are you going to solve it? If you know, tell them. Anybody can say "Don't worry. Trust me." A successful guerrilla shows credibility. Deliver it by citing testimonials, professional credentials, or media coverage.

  Don't hesitate to include details on your solution's ease or affordability. Include anecdotes about how your solution has helped others. This is the heart of the letter, so be sure to tell the whole story.

- Testimonials. Nothing sells like a testimonial. And it doesn't have to be from Michael Jordan. Sincere, unpaid applause from somebody the prospect knows will cost you nothing and reap big rewards.

  Include the names and phone numbers of people who have used and liked your product. One of the greatest mysteries of all is why people write "References available upon request" on their résumés. If your references are great, name them.

- Bonus. Everybody likes a bargain, such as buy one, get one free. A company that markets beds to hospitals offers a free television with every $4,000 purchase. The TV sits at the nurses' station, and the nurses are the ones who make the buying decision.

  You never know what will push a prospect into becoming a customer. Add little nudges in the form of extras, like free service or a monogrammed carrying case.

- Guarantee. You've used testimonials and news coverage to convince your targets you're a real person. Make the most of it. Give them an iron-clad, money-back guarantee. Eliminate the fear of purchasing by eliminating the risk that they'll be unhappy with your product.

- Incentive to act. It's human nature to hate missing out on a good deal. It's also human nature to procrastinate. Give your prospect a solid rea-

TIP! Marketers tend to spend too much time worrying about the content and style of their direct mail letters. The list is far and away the most important component, followed by the offer. The creative aspect is a poor third.

son to act immediately. A freelancer could offer a 5% discount on orders filed before the end of the month, pointing out that as a copywriter, your schedule is full, and next month might be too late.

- Ask for action. You didn't write this letter just to pass the time. What do you want your prospects to do right now? Take your phone call? Set up a time to meet? Return the enclosed stamped envelope? Tell them exactly what to do. Explain why they need to do it now. And then make it easy for them to do.

- Postscript. Research shows that the most read portion of any direct mail letter is a P.S. In your P.S. you can talk about a notable testimonial or a special deal or mention some other salient fact that will encourage the prospect to read the rest of the letter.

Kevin Knight, the president of home-based Knight Marketing Communications Inc. in Dallas, uses a postscript to personalize letters sent to prospects and media contacts. If he's sending out copies of a magazine or newspaper article, he'll use a more or less standard cover letter. But then he'll add a P.S., such as "The third paragraph ought to be particularly interesting to you."

- Enclosures. Consider enclosing good-looking, convincing brochures, business cards, videotapes, or other material that will help your letter. Be careful about this, though. It's easy for someone to skip the letter and jump straight to the brochure, which can sidetrack your efforts.

Consider enclosing an audio tape that gives the listener a free insight into your area of expertise. She can listen in the car, and you've got a captive audience as long as the tape is rolling. But be sure that the tape is informative, not just sales material.

MAKING THE MOST OF MAILING LISTS

Your list is the most important part of your mail campaign. The right list means a profit, while a mediocre list is a license to burn money.

Not all businesses can profit from a mailing aimed at just fifty or a hundred people. Sooner or later, businesses that serve a large audience consider renting mailing lists. Luckily, you can get a list for an amazing number of detailed categories.

Lists are obtained through list brokers. You can find them in the Business-to-business Yellow Pages under Mailing Lists or in a book called the *SRDS Mailing List Directory*, available at most libraries. Call a couple of brokers and ask for their free catalogs. Study them to get an idea of the price, service, and features you can expect. Expect to pay about ten cents a name for the lists that you rent.

Demand precision! *Reader's Digest* and the Lillian Vernon catalog are happy to mail to almost anyone. But you need to mail to only your best prospects. If your core audience is women in Manhattan licensed to carry guns, you can find that list — a bargain at $300.

Types of Lists.

Compiled lists are names culled from phone books, association memberships, and the like. Many big mailers use these large, rather shapeless lists, but used properly, they can be good starting points for guerrillas.

Allen Harpham, a midwestern computer consultant, has mailed flyers and brochures to local government agencies in Nebraska and Kansas advertising his new commercial software. His list came from the State Building Association. The response was strong enough to turn a part-time home-based business into a full-time occupation.

Response lists are people who responded to previous mailings. These can be valuable because they indicate a group responsive to mailings. For example, you can find a list of men, age 30 to 40, living in Texas, who bought a book on incorporating a small business in the last six months. This is a strong list because it has no fictional addresses, escaped convicts, or misfiled names. Every person has shown an interest by spending money.

Business lists have been created by other business-to-business marketers. They tend to have more details than consumer lists. If you need a name, title, and company location for a mailing, you should find it on one of these lists.

House lists are put together by marketers, not brokers or list rental agencies. The very best lists, they are almost impossible to rent through a broker. Instead, you'll have to find one by trading with a fellow entrepreneur. For example, a graphic artist might approach a typesetting house and offer to trade lists. The typesetter gets a referral and is able to send a letter to the companies that use the graphic designer. In exchange, the designer reaches the type users. Each one wins.

TIP! Keep constant and regular contact with people on your mailing list. Send out birthday and holiday cards. Send a coupon good for 10% off their next purchase. Send a thank-you note to anyone who makes a particularly large purchase. Clip newspaper articles and send them to anyone who might find them of interest.

We recently saw a piece of direct mail from a home-based computer business services company. The envelope copy certainly attracted our attention: "Twenty businesses you can run from your home with a computer" and "How would you like to earn $30,000 part-time in twelve weeks?"

Make Your Own Mailing List.

The best list for your business will undoubtedly be one you build yourself. Collect information from customers at every opportunity. Any interaction is a chance to collect a name, address, and phone number. Ever bought anything from Radio Shack? The cashier probably asked you to put your address on the receipt, which may have seemed strange if you were simply buying batteries. But that was how the Radio Shack catalog showed up in your mailbox a few months later.

Suggestion boxes may not yield good ideas, but if you ask for an address on the suggestion slip, it could help fill a list. Federal law says those warranty cards you send in for your stereo or refrigerator have no legal bearing, but they're a great way to learn who's buying what. Subscribers to a newsletter are top prospects for marketing mailings. So are people who drop business cards in a bowl in hopes of winning a drawing.

Camp Arowhon tripled its response from camp fairs by encouraging kids to fill out an entry form to win a free summer at camp. Of course, every entry was a qualified prospect. The cost of giving away one summer at camp was dwarfed by the response from hundreds of targeted prospects.

Stay in Touch.

Making a sales pitch isn't the only reason to write to a customer or prospect. Use your mailing list to send birthday and holiday cards or to make other regular contact. Send thank-yous or even small gifts after big purchases.

Postcards are a great way to keep in touch. They're cheap, and you don't have to write very much, so they're quick to create. Buy some funky postcards and send a few out every day. You'll be surprised at the positive feedback you get.

One successful guerrilla sends postcards to people who call his toll-free voice mail system but don't order anything. Once, he mailed out 3,600 cards on the second of December. By the fifth, the phone was ringing. Through the end of the year, that one mailing generated $27,000 in sales.

ALWAYS TEST

One of direct mail's strengths over other marketing methods is that it can be tested. If a mailing works with 250 random names from a larger list, the odds are it will work with the entire list. Whether or not your mother-in-law likes the color of the envelope, if your test works, the mailing will work.

The first step in successful testing is to keep accurate records. Every mailing you do should be a "split test." Change one variable in half your mailing and see which half does better. Then discard the loser and test something else.

Elements you can test include color versus black-and-white, price, letter length, delivery method, mailing list, tone, free bonuses, deadlines, and even the type of stamps you use. Don't try to test more than one element in each letter — you won't know which change was responsible for the success of the mailing.

Here's a simple way to track the responses to different ads and flyers. Put a different telephone number on each one. Noting the number of calls to each number makes it easy to track the response. Alternatively, you can put a code number, in small print, on the bottom of the return envelope.

> David Wood, a home-based writer catering to the construction industry, sends a direct mail package to his best prospects. Each package costs him almost $15 to produce and mail and contains everything from samples of his newsletters, articles, and sample work. People often ask him how he can afford to send out such an expensive piece. His answer? "How can I afford not to?" He sends the package only to his most qualified leads, people who are responding either to his newsletter or ad in the *New England Real Estate Journal*, requesting more information. One or two additional jobs a year pay for the whole thing.

BYPASS ORDINARY MAIL

Using overnight mail instead of regular mail is one of the most powerful ways to draw attention to your mailing. After all, what mass mailer is going to use anything but the cheapest available delivery method? If you do anything at all impressive, your message can't help but be perceived as different, more important, worth opening, reading, and perhaps responding to.

Take a look at UPS, Federal Express, or Priority Mail. They may cost less than you think, especially if your volume is over a hundred pieces at a time. It's certainly worth a test.

DO YOU HAVE A BUSINESS PLAN YET?

PLEASE LET US HEAR FROM YOU

Several months ago you requested information on our services. Since we h
from you in awhile, we'd appreciate it if you would take just a few minute
the status of your business plan.

❏ My business plan is completed.

❏ My plan is in progress but not yet complete.

❏ I can't seem to get started.

❏ I don't think I need one.

Would you like to continue to receive information from us from time to t

❏ Please keep in touch with me. I may need your services in the futu

❏ Please do not send me any more information.

Name_____ Company_____

Comments/Suggestions:

DETACH AND RETURN TO LAYTON & CO. TODAY!

Home-based business plan writer Marcia Layton uses a three-tier direct mail campaign. Initially she sends a cover letter and brochure to prospects who call her. If they are still interested after receiving the brochure, she sends out a complete packet of information and news clippings. She follows that up several weeks later with this postcard mailing (two of three perforated sections shown here).

DATA BASE PUBLISHING

Data base output is normally associated with reams of monotonous computer printouts and terse reports. Formatting the output from these printouts and reports into attractive, readable documents is a time-consuming and labor-intensive activity. Previously, the automation of such a formatting process required specialized programming and an extensive knowledge by the programmer of both the Data Base Management System (DBMS) and the target page layout program.

This no longer needs to be the case. Answerin[g] requirements of the publishing community, softw[are] developers have written software that greatly enha[nce] the ability to query databases and format the outp[ut] directly into page layout programs. Implementing a capability can greatly reduce the time it takes to publish a data-intensive document.

Publishing data bases is no longer synonymou[s] with producing massive printed volumes. With com[puters] in almost every office, many businesses are now publishing their data bases to electronic media, su[ch as] CD-ROM. This offers reductions in printing cos[ts,] reductions in shipping costs, and rapid productio[n] schedules. It also reduces paper waste and can o[ften] enhance the usability of the published informatio[n by] implementing electronic retrieval mechanisms.

Data bases need not be limited to alphanum[eric] fields. Many DBMSs support a wide variety of [data] types, to include such things as pictures and soun[d. For] example, a business might scan pictures or drawi[ngs of] its products and store them with the associated p[roduct] description and price information. An associatio[n might] store a member's photograph with other relevant m[ember] ship data. In either case, this information could th[en be] extracted and automatically formatted to produ[ce a] paper or electronic document — a parts list or mem[ber] ship directory.

If you have questions about how to publish y[our] data or need help designing or even managing a d[ata] base, give us a call. We have years of experien[ce] working with a variety of DBMSs on different plat[forms.] Let us help you maximize the use of the informati[on] you've painstakingly gathered.

2194 Conover Circle, Oregon, WI 53575-1[908]
Tel: 608.835.7227 Fax: 608.835.7224

SCRIBE SHOP

PLAIN PAPER TYPESETTING

We were all amazed with the introduction of the first laser printers. Compared to typewriters and dot matrix printers, the output quality was phenomenal. The ability to rapidly and inexpensively proof pages composed on desktop computers led to the birth of desktop publishing.

The laser printer revolutionized the quality and readability of business communications and presentations. However, with a resolution of 300 dots per inch (dpi), laser printers did not have the output quality to satisfy the prepress needs of the professional design and publishing communities. Output from the laser printer could not really be considered "camera-ready". It was used only to proof pages composed on the computer before sending the files to a high-resolution output device, such as an imagesetter, to render the camera-ready artwork.

Advances in laser imaging technology have greatly improved printer output quality. Finer grades of toner, improved controller firmware, and specialized print engines have enabled the manufacture of printers with 1200 x 1200 dpi print resolutions. With 1,440,000 dots per square inch, compared to the 90,000 available to 300 dpi printers, true plain paper typesetting is now a reality.

Plain paper typesetters do have certain limitations. While they really shine in the production of camera-ready type and line art, when compared to image-setters, they fall short in the reproduction of halftones (photos). This is because they use a single dot size on a grid to compose an image, while an imagesetter has greater flexibility in dot placement, an ability to vary dot size, and higher available resolution options.

On the right jobs, a *considerable* amount of money can be saved by employing plain paper typesetting over imagesetting electronically composed pages. While imagesetter output is measured in dollars per page, laser output is measured in pennies. Ask your designer whether plain paper typesetting is appropriate for your next project.

This page was set on a plain paper typesetter.

SCRIBE SHOP

2194 Conover Circle, Oregon, WI 53575-1908
Tel: 608.835.7227 Fax: 608.835.7224

Here are two examples of the envelope stuffers that Donna and Scott Lewein use to promote their home-based desktop publishing business. See their story on page 92.

7 NEWSLETTERS
A GREAT GUERRILLA COMMUNICATION TOOL

AS THE HEAD OF A HOME-BASED BUSINESS, you are the whole operation — mailroom, writer, marketer, industry expert, accountant, and CEO. Because you're on the front lines, you know more about your industry than almost anyone at a larger company. You understand the trends, you talk directly to customers, and you have experience with product creation and in dealing with bankers. In short, you've combined the skills of a dozen people in one expert guerrilla.

How can you make the most of your knowledge? By publishing your own newsletter. We're not talking *Citizen Kane* here. The goal is not to generate lots of subscribers or even to make a profit. A small, focused, low-cost, promotional newsletter mailed to potential and existing customers is a great way to leverage your personal strengths.

A newsletter gives you yet another way to show your customers who you are and how you can help them. It keeps your name and personality in front of exactly the right people. It gives you the opportunity to become a source of information as well as a source of products and services. If you can do that, you'll gain respect and loyalty from your customers.

Obviously, a newsletter isn't the perfect tool for everyone; a supermarket, movie theater, or 7-Eleven isn't going to generate enough profit from any one customer to justify sending out a free newsletter. But if you're targeting a select group and selling a product with a big price tag, a newsletter may be what you need.

A public relations wizard who works with toy companies, Stew Reads, talks and thinks about toys every day. He knows which companies are introducing which products, what's doing well at Toys "R" Us, and which factories in Hong Kong are having trouble. Think that toy executives want to get their hands on that information? Stew provides such juicy tidbits while keeping his own name in front of an ideal target market, all by sharing his knowledge in a monthly newsletter.

Many home-based business people have similarly valuable knowledge to share. Perhaps you're a copywriter, specializing in direct mail advertising. As part of your job, you study the hundreds of pieces of junk mail you get every week. You've probably seen just about everything from the very good to the very bad. It's not hard to imagine that your clients and prospects would enjoy a digest of the latest direct mail pieces — information they don't have time to glean on their own.

Ivan Levison is one of the nation's top direct mail copywriters. He specializes in writing letters that promote computer software to end users. Once a month he sends everyone on his mailing list a one-page (two-sided) newsletter that gives away all his secrets. Crazy? Like a fox.

People don't hire Ivan because they need his secrets. They hire him because his ability to turn those secrets into successful direct mail letters is unparalleled. And the newsletter makes that clear. In addition to techniques that work, his newsletter contains examples of his most effective work.

After receiving Ivan's newsletter for a few months, people not only come to expect it, they look forward to it. Readers know they'll learn from each issue. They respect Ivan, and many eventually become clients.

THE ANATOMY OF A NEWSLETTER

A newsletter is neither a newspaper nor a direct mail letter but something in between. It comes out regularly and has a standard format. Focused on a specific industry or market, it has the distinct individual flair of the guerrilla who publishes it.

Newsletters are usually two, four, or eight pages of letter-size paper, but they can also be a single sheet printed on both sides. Long or short, they're packed with timely, brief information that your target audience will find useful for solving problems — but won't find anywhere else.

A successful newsletter is well designed and easy to look at. It may include photographs and illustrations along with text. But it is not expensive to produce and it doesn't have to be a multimedia extravagan-

 TIP! Be succinct. Your newsletter does not have to be long to have an impact. Most people see a newsletter as something they can read quickly to get some useful information.

za. If you use guerrilla techniques and do much of the work yourself, you can write, design, print, and deliver it for less than 50¢ a copy.

A newsletter is a great way to reach new prospects and to stay in touch with customers. Although delivered by mail, it can't really be considered "direct mail" because of key differences.

Predictability.

A predictable schedule is the biggest difference. A good newsletter is as regular as clockwork.

Whether it arrives every Monday or on the fifteenth of alternate months, it's critical that it be there when the reader expects it.

Newsletters Are Read First, Not Last.

A newsletter should be enjoyable and informative. If it's well done, the people on your mailing list will eagerly await each issue. How eagerly? Many newsletters start out as marketing giveaways and turn into profit-generating subscription products.

The Motivation Is to Tell, Not Sell.

Unlike direct mail, the goal is not to get a sale with each newsletter you send out. But over time your newsletter will build a strong enough relationship with prospects that they will feel comfortable buying from you.

For a direct mail campaign, the home-based marketing consultant Ilise Benun writes a letter discussing her prospect's most pressing problems, presents her qualifications to solve them, and then requests an appointment, phone conversation, or outright sale. In her newsletter, "The Art of Self-Promotion," Ilise offers pure information. For instance, she tells readers four basic messages to put on an answering machine to turn it into a marketing tool — free know-how without the sales pitch.

Ilise is still marketing, of course. She's building credibility and forming relationships instead of going for immediate sales. The results can be even better with an indirect approach. Ilise received so much interest in and business from her newsletter that three years ago she turned it into a self-liquidating subscription publication.

Act Objectively, Even Recommending Other Products and Services.

Although you would never send out a direct mail piece in which you recommend a competitor's product, sometimes it pays to do just that in your newsletter. A monthly newsletter keeps Mike Lee in touch with the customers of his printing service bureau. Filled with ways for people to make the most of prepress service bureaus and printers, it also describes alternatives to high-cost typesetting. Mike's tips may help readers cut their overall prepress expenditures. They could even cost him some sales volume. But Mike knows that if he's positioned himself as an unbiased adviser, he'll make up those sales and more.

WHAT A NEWSLETTER CAN DO FOR YOU

Before you start a newsletter, decide why you're writing it. A newsletter can give you a lot: more credibility, better access to decision-makers, a way to announce new products, and stronger customer ties, all of which contribute directly to your bottom line. Let's look at these points.

Credibility.
Credibility is critical for the home-based guerrilla. Remember, trust is the key to overcoming the fear that many people have about buying something.

If you publish a newsletter on a special subject, you will become known as a bona fide expert. This can lead to other work that gives you more exposure and a still higher profile as an expert. The longer you publish your newsletter, the more trusted your name will become.

Kimberly Stanséll, the successful home-based business information broker in Los Angeles, attributes much of her success to her quarterly newsletter, "Bootstrappin' Entrepreneur." Since she started it three years ago, her reputation as a marketing and research expert has grown by leaps and bounds. In fact, the editors at *Home Office Computing* magazine were so impressed that they asked her to write an article on small business. That exposure led to a job creating a newsletter for US West. Stanséll was just as good before "Bootstrappin' Entrepreneur" appeared, but nobody knew. Afterward, she had credibility to burn.

The credibility you gain with a newsletter often leads to public speaking and consulting, two outlets that can further your reputation in your field — and they pay quite well. Ilise Benun, who publishes "The Art of Self-Promotion," gets three or four requests per season to speak on self-marketing. Most come from people who have seen her newsletter. Ilise started speaking for free, but now that she charges for her time, she's opened up a whole new source of revenue.

One of the beauties of newsletters is that they benefit the marketer

TIP! Your newsletter is a selling tool, but it has to educate the reader, too. Don't just fill it with advertising or you will lose your reader.

The newsletter used by Mike Lee to communicate with and educate his customers about the imagesetting business.

more and more the longer they've been around. To get the maximum bang for your buck, be prepared to publish your newsletter for years. If you're lucky, it will become so useful that you can start charging your readers for it. That's exactly what happened to both Ilise and Kimberly. Each newsletter started as a free promotional tool. Demand grew so much that both women now charge a nominal fee for subscriptions so they can break even.

Reaching Decision-Makers.

Having trouble getting through to the people who decide whether you'll get the business? Ordinary direct mail often gets opened by gatekeepers, but newsletters are treated more like magazines and newspapers. They get more respect. A newsletter can put your name, face, and words in front of people who would never glance at a sales brochure.

New Products Pipeline.

A regular newsletter is an ideal way to update customers if you have a steady stream of new products or services. Alan Shulman, who manufactures the battery-operated sump pump called the Basement Watchdog, considers his most important customers the retailers who carry his product — shelf space equals sales for Alan. He needed a way to remind them about his product, so he began publishing a newsletter, "The Rainy Day Gazette." He mails it to retailers as a way to educate them about the new products and features of his company, Glentronics. Two stories from a recent issue are "Basement Watchdog Uses Less Than 6¢ of Electricity per Day to Maintain Its Battery at Full Charge" and "Glentronics Service Department Expands." Notice that Alan carefully walks the fine line between newsletter and sales brochure. If all you do in your newsletter is try to sell, your reader will feel cheated. A newsletter implies news, and if you fail to provide any useful information, you run the risk of generating ill will.

Building Relationships.

Building relationships with prospective customers and keeping in touch with existing ones is another benefit of publishing a newsletter. What guerrillas wouldn't want to develop a sense of community among their customers? Or encourage word-of-mouth referrals? A newsletter can accomplish that.

Dawn Orford, a trade show consultant who works out of her home in Penfield, New York, publishes a monthly newsletter, "Exhibit Marketing News." In a few short pages, it dispenses exhibition advice in articles like "Dos and Don'ts for Booth Attendees" and "Exhibit Memorability: Getting Attendees to Remember You." It carries a schedule of her trade show marketing seminars as well as an updated schedule of trade shows around the country. Dawn literally stamps the newsletter with her own image by running a picture of herself in every issue.

Even though Dawn provides a lot of useful information, she never forgets the real purpose of her newsletter. She often has a section of testimonials, and she always includes a detachable business reply card that people can use to request more information about her services.

According to Dawn, "For the price of copies and postage, I keep my name and face in front of my clients and prospects throughout the year without having to bug them on the phone. I report our customer satisfaction results. I promote our public seminars, and with informative articles, I whet their appetite for more information and better trade show results. It establishes image and credibility. It builds trust, and the photo builds the relationship."

> Every quarter, David Woods, a home-based writer catering to the construction industry, mails his promotional newsletter "Words from Woody," to the 2,000 people on his mailing list. He pastes a four-color sticker picturing himself with his two dogs on the nameplate of each one. It only costs him pennies, but it makes a big impact. He often follows up the newsletter with a telephone call. If he tells the secretary that he's the one who sends "that funny newsletter with the dogs on it," he's more likely to be put through.

WHAT TO FOCUS ON

The first questions you need to ask are: "Why should customers read my newsletter? What's in it for them?"

Go to the source for answers. Get a few of your best clients or top prospects to tell you what interests them. If they read other newsletters, what do they like or dislike about them? What would they like to see? Do they have problems that nobody is addressing?

Even better, invite them to help create your newsletter. Many of your customers will be flattered if you ask them to write articles. No doubt some are proud of their knowledge and eager to share it. Why not accommodate them and save yourself work and money at the same time?

Recruiting readers as writers also makes your newsletter a two-way communications tool. Use letters to the editor, guest editorials, reader surveys, and other features that involve response from readers. Everybody loves to feel listened to. A guerrilla encourages people to talk back.

A Florida guerrilla who sells business machines markets with a monthly newsletter. In one issue, he wanted to explain a few facts about the hidden costs of doing business with his low-priced superstore competitors. He asked one of his customers to write down his thoughts about lack of service, inconvenient packaging, and some superstore failings. With the customer's permission, he edited the notes into a great article for his newsletter. His message came across more objectively from a third-party point of view. As a bonus, he strengthened ties with that customer, who was thrilled to see his name in print.

NEWSLETTER CONTENT

No need to reinvent the wheel. There are lots of great newsletters; there are even books filled with award-winning newsletter designs. Here are some features any home-based newsletter publisher should consider.

Photos.

Photographs are indispensable in announcing new products. They help explain how-to stories. Include photographs of readers, customers, and prospects at every opportunity. Go to trade shows and conventions and photograph the crowd. Include a customer's photograph in every issue. Don't forget your own picture. People will recall a face before they remember a name. Dawn Orford considers including your own picture in a newsletter one of the five rules of marketing. If you have employees, run their pictures to introduce new personnel or the Employee of the Month.

It doesn't cost very much to include photographs. If you're using a computer, you can add a scanner to your setup for about $500, and the printing costs about the same as a newsletter with only text. If you don't want to buy a scanner, ask your printer to strip in the photo for you.

 TIP! Don't make your design too fancy. The most important thing is legibility. If your newsletter is hard to follow or difficult to read, most people will just skip it altogether.

Letters.

You may have to go to great lengths to inspire readers to write to your newsletter. Put a boxed paragraph in every issue that says: "We love to hear from our readers. Write to us with your comments, complaints, criticism, and praise. We'll publish as many letters as we can." Why? Letters are a true guerrilla tool: personal, interactive, focused. They're the kind of thing big companies won't and can't do. And there's nothing wrong with printing a critical letter — especially if you have a new policy or a good response that addresses the criticism.

Contests.

Offering a prize is one sure way to get feedback. The prize doesn't have to be a new car or a week in Waikiki. A free subscription, a sample, or simple recognition (like the winner's photo in your newsletter) may be enough. Entry requirements could be as easy as filling out a postcard or faxing a form. They could be as complicated as writing a fifty-word description of why your reader likes your product. People love contests, and the interaction builds your relationship. No matter who else wins, you win, too.

Profiles.

As a newsletter publisher, you can let your subscribers tell their stories, brag about their families, and even promote their own businesses in print. Pick one subscriber to profile in every issue. Choose them at random, through a drawing or when you hear of an interesting person. Give a few facts such as name, company, job, and family details. Run their pictures. You'll flatter them, help them in their own networking, and come across as a human business person who cares about customers.

Statistics.

Your newsletter becomes indispensable if it helps readers sort valuable tidbits from the torrent of information we're all exposed to. If you see a published report about some government statistics or industry research that might interest your readers, select the most relevant nuggets. Print them in a brief, easily digestible form. Or generate your own statistics from surveying readers, experts, or other companies in your industry.

Predictions.

Use your newsletter to talk about industry trends. Subtly point out ways in which your business may be helpful to people. These aren't exercises in ESP. They're opportunities to demonstrate your knowledge and experience. One home-based guerrilla stockbroker calls his forecast feature "Where to Invest Now" and uses it to predict trends in the market. A lawyer specializing in medical liability forecasts the likely effects of a new law regulating pharmacists. You don't have to be right. Just give your readers a springboard to help them plan or, even better, something to help them think.

Editorials.

Most reporters at traditional publications are told to avoid injecting personal opinions in their writing. As a home-based business person, your strength *is* your ability to care passionately about your customers. Express it! Feature a regular editorial page that gives your opinion about issues facing your industry and your customers. Or focus on personal matters, as Jan Melnik does with the quarterly newsletter for her home-based secretarial service. Jan offers plenty of shop talk, but she also includes a personal column in which she chats about whatever is on her mind. What better way to create an image of herself as a real person rather than a bland, faceless corporation.

Interviews.

If it's not easy to get readers to write to you, you can still get their names, pictures, and words in the newsletter. Call them up and interview them. If you're introducing a new product, ask people to tell you how they plan to use it. If you need reaction to an industry issue or tips on solving nagging problems, a few phone calls should provide you with a wealth of information and a tighter relationship with everyone you talk with.

Don't use interviews as sales calls in disguise. You'll do nothing but alienate prospects and customers. Instead, flatter them by asking their opinion; give them a chance to make pronouncements on the industry. Save your sales call for the next month, after the newsletter comes out.

Soft Sell.

Resist the temptation to fill your newsletter with hard-sell information. If you toot your own horn too much without giving your reader anything of value, your newsletter will fail. Use a more subtle approach. Always include a way for readers to contact you if they want more information. Offer a free sample of your services or include a column of testimonials from satisfied customers, as Dawn Orford does. Jan Melnik usually includes either a coupon or a special bonus that will help readers with their business in every issue of her newsletter.

EXHIBIT MARKETING NEWS

NEWS AND IDEAS FOR TRADE SHOW EXHIBIT MANAGERS

Published by Orford & Associates, Rochester, NY

Exhibit Memorability - Part I
Getting Attendees to Remember You

Getting attendees to remember your booth is invaluable. It can influence purchasing decisions as well as build a long company awareness.

According to the Trade Show Bureau, size is the primary physical factor in getting attendees to remember you. However, if you cannot adjust your size, try enhancing the other six of the top seven physical memorability factors of exhibiting.

1. Attendee product interest. According to the Trade Show Bureau, the level of attendee interest in the products and services being displayed is the number one physical reason, other than size, for getting attendees to remember your company.

This means that you have to be sure to exhibit at the right shows, the shows where attendees are interested in your products. Additionally, it is critical that you create awareness and curiosity before the show.

2. Product demonstrations. Next in rank in memorability is demonstrations and presentations. Demonstrations and presentations draw attendees to your booth and helps them remember your products and services.

Research also shows that demonstrations and presentations given by professional narrators were the most effective.

3. Exhibit color and design. The third-ranked physical memorability factor is the overall design and color scheme of your exhibit.

Exhibit design, color, and overall message should be effective in drawing attendees into your booth.

For those businesses where demonstrations are impossible, design becomes an even more crucial exhibiting factor.

Part II of this article will be published in the next issue.

ROUTE TO:
☐ _____
☐ _____
☐ _____

IN THIS ISSUE

♦ Exhibit Memorability - Part I

♦ Clients Give O&A a 4.0!

♦ Calendar of Upcoming Shows

♦ Do's & Don'ts for Staffers

♦ Quote of the Quarter

♦ Seminar Schedule

Dawn Orford's "Exhibit Marketing News."

WHO WRITES IT?

The ideal newsletter is written by the guerrilla. No one else knows exactly what his or her home-based business is all about and what it has to offer. To make the most of the guerrilla's ability to focus, the newsletter should seem personal, not mass-produced.

Can you imagine someone other than Jan Melnik writing the personal essay in her secretarial service's newsletter? It's how Jan differentiates herself from the impersonal, inhuman, giant temporary services she competes against. However, not every guerrilla has the time, talent, or inclination to produce a newsletter. A poorly written, poorly edited, poorly designed newsletter is an embarrassment. Better skip it all together or find a professional to provide a quality touch.

Professional editors and producers create dozens of newsletters a year. But they aren't cheap. Hiring outside help will increase your costs substantially. Good writers charge $25 an hour and up. Figure a couple thousand dollars per issue to have someone do your entire newsletter, less if you do part of it yourself.

Before you send out your first issue, print six copies and show them to your lawyer, your accountant, a few customers, and a friend. Ask them for an honest opinion before you proceed.

IMAGE IS EVERYTHING

Everyone judges a book by its cover, and the same is true for newsletters. If it doesn't look good, it won't work. (Note: looking good doesn't always mean looking expensive. A simple, clean newsletter can be quite effective.)

In the old days, many newsletters were typed on a manual typewriter, with headlines all in capital letters. Then they were photocopied, offset-printed, or even mimeographed, and mailed out.

Today we are in the age of desktop publishing. Fast computers, sharp displays, powerful software, and cheap laser printers allow anybody to produce a newsletter with a clever layout, appealing type, and clear illustrations. Fortunately, there is a guerrilla solution that will let you keep up with these advances on a limited budget.

 TIP! Reduce the cost of producing your newsletter by creating a self-mailing piece. You'll save the cost of envelopes and the time needed to stuff them.

The Guerrilla Solution.

First, find a newsletter you love. Go to the library or get a directory of newsletters and send for some samples. Look for those that stand out as attractive and unique. Make sure you don't choose a newsletter in your own industry, market, or service area. The last thing you want to do is come up with a design that looks exactly like another newsletter your client is already getting.

Once you've found a few candidates, get some help. Talk over your selections with a desktop publisher. This professional can translate the model newsletter into a template for your own desktop publishing program.

Like a form, a template comes with special formatting, choices for headline type, boxes and borders, and all the other elements that make a newsletter look special, unified, and attractive. Once you have the template, you'll be able to create future issues yourself simply by filling in the words and illustrations.

A word of caution. Each issue will necessarily be a little bit different. But don't stray too far from your template. You want a consistent look. Like an old friend, your newsletter should seem familiar. Unless you're trying to sell people on your amazing design skills, use the same template for every issue, with a minimum of tampering.

Another way to cut costs, maximize appeal, and maintain consistency is to design a color masthead. Your local quick printer can use colored ink and colored paper to create a sharp, snazzy look — and the cost is amazingly low if you print a large quantity. Have enough printed to last you for several issues. Then, when it's time to publish the newsletter, you can print the black-and-white copy on the already-printed color masthead. You save time and money and end up with a professional-looking piece for half the cost.

A good laser printer is ideal for running off proofs of your newsletter to see what it looks like. If your circulation is less than 100 copies, that may be all you need. Once you pass that level, use professional offset printing. It costs only a few cents a copy for any kind of volume. And it will make your newsletter's image the equal of the best.

MAKING IT SOUND GOOD

A newsletter needs a name that expresses its benefits to the readers, isn't too focused on you or your product, and — please! — isn't too cute.

Short, simple names are best. "Bootstrappin' Entrepreneur." "The

Art of Self-Promotion." "Exhibit Marketing News." No one is going to have trouble understanding what these newsletters are about.

It's tempting to use your newsletter's name as an advertisement for your business or yourself. Resist it. Your newsletter should introduce your business and carry news about it. But it should be about your customers' needs, not yours.

Ilise Benun could have called her newsletter "The Ilise Benun Quarterly." "The Art of Self-Promotion" is better because it promises her customers information they need to know, not just stuff about Ilise Benun. It's unique, memorable, and straightforward.

As for the content, keep it short. No article should be longer than a page. There's no need to write entire articles…you can separate different thoughts by ellipses.

Your newsletter is a reflection of you and your company, so make sure it is accurate. Hire an editor to catch spelling mistakes, errors in grammar, and lapses in logic so they don't embarrass you. Not all editors are created equal, however. Yours should understand your newsletter's goals, be able to hear the "voice" you want, and have suitable experience.

GETTING IT OPENED

The envelope your newsletter arrives in should be like a teenager at a dance — determined and ready to do almost anything to attract attention. Here's how to get your envelope opened.

- Find a stand-out envelope.
- Write compelling copy.
- Use unusual stamps.
- Try labels that draw the eye.
- Send it to the right people to start with.
- Or don't use an envelope — make your newsletter a self-mailer.

Stand-Out Envelopes.

The other day a large envelope made of rough purple paper arrived. It was from a Washington, D.C., newsletter publisher who clearly knew what he was doing. In the dull pile of smooth and white bond envelopes, his newsletter package stood out like a grape in a bowl of oatmeal. It was quickly brought to the top and ripped open.

Select your envelope with an eye to having the same effect. Play with the color, the shape, and the size.

Stamp Ideas.

Another thing about that purple envelope that caught the eye was the postage. Most solicitations have an offset-printed postage-paid emblem or a red postage-meter imprint. There's a good chance these boring, dime-a-dozen missives will be tossed into the read-later pile, if not into the trash.

This purple newsletter had two oversize 29-cent stamps featuring bright tropical fish. They were stuck on crooked and upside down. A 40-cent stamp and a 3-cent stamp were half-plastered on top. It's hard to imagine a more amateurish-looking job. Did it convince the recipient that this was a private, one-of-a-kind communication from a real person? Instantly!

If your newsletter is going to a senior executive at a company with a formal corporate culture, you might tone down your stamp display. But the fact remains: postage can do more than get a newsletter delivered. It can get it opened.

Label Ideas.

Even the way you address the envelope affects its chances of being noticed and opened. An envelope with a laser-printed address showing through a hole in the front has "mass-mail" written all over it.

Try writing the address by hand. With a green pen!

Envelope Copy Ideas.

Don't stop with the stamp and label. A well-written line on the outside of your envelope will increase the chances of its being opened. Here are some examples:

- Inside: The Pet Supplier's Bird Care Monthly

- Your Copy of Printing for Profit

- Shareware Quarterly: A Newsletter for Part-Time Programmers

These very straightforward teasers convey exactly what readers will find inside the envelope. Increase interest with a teaser that focuses more on emotional pull than on flat statement, such as:

- Want to know today's best moneymaking ideas? Look inside.

 Have someone else edit your newsletter. Ruthlessly. Check it for spelling, too.

THE BRIEFING

September 1994

Direct Marketing News and Views

New York -- Chase Manhattan Bank has seen an almost 1 percent acquisition rate using a compiled data base of 500,000 affluent prospects to target its local offices' direct mail offers for mortgages.

♦ ♦ ♦

The best and biggest month for direct marketers is December. So begin preparing now for your December mailing.

♦ ♦ ♦

Boca Raton, FL -- Dunhill International List Co. Inc. is unveiling its 695,488-name Business Owners at-Home file.

This list is full of small-retail and service-business owners in the U.S. However, professionals have not been included. Call 407/347-0200.

How To Make Your Mailing Successful

There are a number of things you can do to assure yourself of a successful mailing.

Of course, having excellent well-prepared copy is one of the most important. But you can have the best copy in the world, and if you don't send your mailing to the best target market or put your ad in the publication that goes to that target market, you won't get the response you expect.

So knowing who your target market is and aiming your copy toward it is number one.

Next, should you personalize? I tell my clients that, in most cases, it pays to do so. Of course, there are times you simply can't afford to. Or for some other reason it would be impractical. But for the most part, personalize if you can.

Don't use labels unless you must. You want your mail piece to look as much like a personal letter as you can.

In most cases, it's best to use First Class postage. But not always. For example, if you're trying to get subscriptions to a publication, usually a bulk rate stamp is best.

Another tip to remember is to sign your letters with medium blue ink. Don't ask me why this is best but it's tested better than anything else

Use a PS whenever you can. BUT, make the PS meaningful because it will be the very first thing the reader will read!

Finally, use a lift letter. That's a little note inside a sealed envelope that says on the outside something like:
"Read only if you've decided not to return the card."

In this lift letter, write a very short but powerful final push to make the prospect lift his or her hand and send the card in, or c or whatever you want him or h to do.

These tips won't ensure your success. But they'll give you n ammunition. And remember, must test, test, test. Don't giv up.

Susanna Hutcheson mails this monthly newsletter to all of the customers and prospects on her mailing list. It has helped establish her credibility in the direct mail advertising industry and has brought her lots of new business as well!

- Your customers could be buying more from you. Here's why.

- Don't Open This Envelope! (If You Don't Want a Surprise.)

There is valuable marketing space between the stamp and the address. Be judicious with teasers, as they can sometimes scream "junk mail." Test various approaches to find out what works, and make the most of it.

WHO GETS YOUR NEWSLETTER?

When you send your newsletter to a list of people already interested in your subject, they will likely open your envelope the first time they see it. Some lists you can create. Some you can rent. Others you already own. For instance:

Build prospect lists. You need to become a name packrat. Whenever you find a lead, add it to your database. Use classified ad respondents. People who ask for samples. People who attend a seminar you hold. People referred by existing subscribers. Trade show visitors who stop by your booth. People who drop business cards in a bowl for a drawing. Almost any interaction between you and customers or prospects is an opportunity to capture a name and address. Try to come up with new ways to create that contact, such as contests and giveaways.

If customers don't reach out to you, reach out to them. Whenever Connecticut desktop publishing and office services guerrilla Jan Melnik reads in the newspaper about people who are doing something interesting, she looks up their address and adds them to the mailing list for one of her two newsletters.

Renting lists. Pick up a copy of *Standard Rate and Data Service* (*SRDS*), the bible of mailing lists (available at your library). You can find everything from the list of 1,243 women in New York City authorized to carry a handgun to the more than 3 million direct mail respondents to an offer for a hair growth elixir. There are literally thousands of lists available, and one may be perfect for your newsletter.

Your customer list. Definitely send your newsletter to the people you already do business with. They often need a gentle reminder that you're still alive and well and as feisty as ever.

SHOULD YOU CHARGE?

If the most important thing a newsletter can do is reach out to people, do you want to charge them for the privilege? It's not always easy to decide.

Jan Melnik may get more marketing benefit from her newsletter because it is a free publication. Actually, it is a controlled-circulation publication, meaning that Melnik sends it without charge to the people she chooses. Controlling her circulation this way makes certain that her message gets to the right market instead of to whomever happens to buy a subscription.

We've discussed how Ilise Benun started her newsletter as a free promotional mailing. After several years of gradual growth, she turned it into a paid subscription publication. After three months of sending his newsletter for free, Chris Beal asks subscribers to pay a small fee to have the mailings continue.

Which approach is right for you? Odds are, you should give it away, at least at first. Later, you may develop such a strong reader response that you can start charging for it.

You'll no doubt lose some readers when you switch. But those who stay will really be committed and interested in what you have to say. You may even wind up picking up extra subscribers if you tack on a price. It's human nature to bestow more prestige on costlier items. Some newsletters sell for $500 or more a year. Who knows, it may become more profitable than the business you're promoting!

ALTERNATIVES TO TRADITIONAL NEWSLETTERS

Regular mail isn't the only way to deliver your newsletter. Electronic delivery via fax or e-mail offers some significant advantages for guerrilla marketers over the old-fashioned postal service, aka snail mail. The key is to know the rules and limitations of modern, high-speed communications.

Faxing a newsletter is days faster than mailing it. And you save on postage, especially if you're faxing locally and local calls are free.

Faxing etiquette requires that you have the permission of the recipient before you fax. This will help overcome a major problem, namely, that faxes often don't get through to their target person.

And remember, faxing is faster, but faxes are considered more disposable than a printed, mailed document. That means your newsletter is less likely to be saved.

You'll also give up a lot in appearance, so you'll have to try extra hard to come up with a good layout that's readable after transmission by fax.

If you decide to go the fax route, investigate a fax board for your computer. For only a couple hundred dollars, it can automatically dial each fax machine at night while you're out. The quality of the faxes it sends will be far better, too.

E-mail is almost free and is delivered instantly right to the computer of the person you're sending it to. You won't need to hassle with layouts, either, since almost all e-mail is sent as unformatted streams of text. Again, you lose the impact of good design if you e-mail your newsletter, so make sure the content is strong.

Why aren't all newsletters sent by e-mail? Not everybody has access to e-mail. If you do, you need to work hard to get e-mail addresses. (There isn't a phone book of e-mail addresses anywhere.) And the etiquette of e-mail, like that of faxing, rules out sending unsolicited newsletters.

For certain markets, e-mail and fax newsletters are well suited. Financial advisers, whose customers insist on absolutely up-to-the-minute market information, find fax sheets ideal. If most of your customers have electronic mailboxes, e-mail can be a solid solution.

8 CLASSIFIED ADS
TARGETED, CHEAP, AND EFFECTIVE ADVERTISING

BARBARA COOLE-RICHMAN WAS DOING FINE selling cotton clothing through her catalog from her Santa Rosa, California, home. Customers loved her products because they contained no chemical additives. She also heard about one mother who ordered her clothing for her disabled child because, with few zippers and other fasteners, it made dressing the child extremely easy.

Barbara wanted to find out how other parents of disabled children would respond. She needed an inexpensive way to test her product in a very specific market. A larger company might have commissioned a lengthy, expensive market study. Barbara chose the guerrilla solution: she placed a small classified ad in *Exceptional Parent* magazine. Before long, she had cracked a whole new market and was generating sales dollars. A nonguerrilla would still be "studying" the market.

Classified advertisements are usually small, without illustration, and grouped by categories determined by the products or services for sale. All computer consultants go in one category, all antiques in another. Because the ads are conveniently "classified," they're read by serious buyers, not just recreational shoppers.

Classified ads offer guerrillas the benefits of low cost, flexibility, precision targeting, and ease in testing. They're not glamorous. Nor are they profitable for advertising agencies, which is one reason that giant marketers generally ignore them. But as many guerrillas have found, they're delightfully productive once you've crafted a winner.

FOUR REASONS TO USE CLASSIFIEDS

Classifieds differ from standard display advertising in several ways, all of which work to a guerilla's advantage.

They Are Unbelievably Inexpensive.

Display ads may cost thousands of dollars to produce. Classified ads incur basically no production cost. There's no photography, no color separation, no printing or ad slick costs. You simply mail or phone in your ad and the publication does the layout and typesetting.

How else can you advertise to nearly 2 million readers for under $200? That's what it costs to place a two-line ad in *Popular Science*, circulation 1.8 million. Many smaller, more highly targeted publications are even less expensive.

Classified advertising is a great way to test a business idea because it's so inexpensive. Remember guerrilla Christian Beal, who sells refurbished Macintosh computers out of his apartment in Florida? Before diving headlong into his business, he tested the waters by placing classifieds in several college newspapers. He worded the ad to make it sound as if he was an individual selling one computer to one person at one university. The response was so overwhelming that he realized there was quite a market for used computers among the university set. Now he uses a variety of marketing tools, from telephone to direct mail. But classified ads are still the backbone of his business.

> Every day, marketing consultant and writer Susanna K. Hutcheson visits clients all over the United States and Europe, yet she never leaves her Wichita home. Susanna built her business primarily on the strength of her classified advertisement on CompuServe, the largest computer online service. Through extensive trial and error, Susanna has determined that a one-line classified draws the most qualified leads for her. She follows up each lead with a well-written, very detailed direct mail letter by e-mail or fax. Susanna expects to earn over $75,000 this year from her travels on the information superhighway.

The Goal Is Action.

The goal of a classified ad is to get the reader to act, by requesting more information or, ideally, by purchasing your product outright. Contrast this with traditional display advertising or other guerrilla tools, such as publicity and newsletters. Classifieds don't build image or brand name. They won't position you as an expert, and they certainly won't help you build customer relationships all on their own. They will, however, get readers to respond directly to you.

High Targetability.

Classifieds might have been invented for guerrillas focusing on niche markets. There is no more precise way to target your marketing. Only the people you want to view your message will see it. By calling or writing to you for more information, they present themselves to you as just the right audience for your product.

So many highly specialized publications run classifieds, you can certainly find a niche to match your market. Guerrilla Marjorie Desgrosseillier wanted to advertise her home-based information broker service. She located the *Corporate Library Update*, a publication that goes to all the librarians of all the big companies all over the country. That's precision targeting. But it gets better. Marjorie's ad appeared in the Information Brokers category of the magazine's classifieds, a place where only corporate librarians specifically looking for information brokers are likely to go.

No matter what or where you're selling — database design to businesses that use FileMaker Pro software or organic lawn care in the Florida panhandle — there is bound to be a publication and category precisely targeted at your market. Few if any other marketing media can make this claim.

Classifieds Hit Motivated Shoppers.

To add to their virtues, classified ads are read almost exclusively by highly motivated shoppers. It's not easy poring over the tiny gray type in a newspaper's classified section. You can bet anyone patient enough to check out the classifieds is ready to buy. You couldn't ask for a better audience.

WHAT CLASSIFIEDS CAN DO FOR YOU

Classified ads have many uses. They can help you build a list for a direct mail, newsletter, or telemarketing campaign. They are excellent for qualifying prospects. They may be able to sell specific products and services all by themselves.

 Make every word count in your classified ad. Using incomplete sentences and abbreviations is fine — but test your ad with a colleague to make sure every word is understandable before you run it.

It is not easy to get people to buy directly from a classified. They are skeptical of sending off their check or credit card number sight unseen. You will have far better success if you use your classified ad to get people interested in what you have to sell. Offer them a brochure, a free trial, or an informational videotape about your product or service. Then, add all of the respondents to your ad to your mailing list and follow up immediately and often.

When Linda Abraham runs classifieds for her home-based graduate school application writing service in the UCLA paper, all she wants from callers is an address. Then she mails her secret weapon: a pamphlet of tips on writing grad school applications and her credentials as a lecturer to preprofessional student groups.

This way of qualifying prospects and following up is often referred to as a two-step selling process. The purpose of your classified ad is to obtain the names, addresses, and phone numbers of interested and motivated buyers, not to sell to them right away. Once someone has responded to your ad, they're more likely to buy your product than if you had just made a cold contact by mail or by phone.

Refurbished Mac salesman Christian Beal is a master at two-step selling. When he advertises in college newspaper classifieds, he just wants one thing: to make his toll-free phone number ring. He doesn't give an address for people to mail a check to. He doesn't even specify precisely what he has to sell (other than a single used Macintosh). All that comes later. It starts with a classified ad that gives him direct contact with a customer.

Computer shoppers who call his toll-free telephone number are funneled into an elaborate voice mail system, which tells them they have reached ReComp, a company that sells refurbished Macintosh computers. The machine records names, numbers, and whatever information the caller offers. Chris reviews his messages (there can be more than a hundred a day) and responds with a letter and product literature. He also sends a phone number people can use to reach him directly.

By the time Chris actually speaks to potential customers, they are ready to buy. They received information from him and know what Chris is all about. More important, they are interested in what Chris has to sell. Classified advertising provides the leverage to help him make the most of his sales time.

Ever see an ad for Coke in the classifieds? Neither have we. Despite

 TIP! Try testing a fax number for a classified response, especially if your classified is aimed at businesses.

the proven effectiveness of classifieds, few large companies advertise there. Classifieds don't fit big-company marketing goals. They're not for image-polishing. They do little to build name recognition. They're not too useful for familiarizing people with complicated new concepts. They're for aiming specific products and services at narrowly defined market niches with the goal of generating a direct response.

WHERE TO RUN YOUR CLASSIFIED AD

There are lots of decisions to make in a classified ad marketing campaign, from pricing to copy to how you'll handle responses. But where to run your ad is the most important decision you'll make. You have a choice among magazines, newspapers, and on-line services.

The key word is target. Linda Abraham wants to reach prospects with two characteristics: (1) They're near UCLA. (2) They plan to apply to graduate school. A classified ad in the UCLA Pre-Professional Advising Office newsletter, which goes to all students interested in applying to professional schools, is a bull's-eye.

A similarly exact match exists for almost any classified concept. If you're trying to reach dashboard designers, try advertising in the trade journal called *Automotive & Transportation Interiors*. Want to target 100,000 office managers? Try the newsletter "Office Systems." If you sell to railroad passengers, make sure you are in *Amtrak Express*, the free publication distributed on Amtrak trains. Stockbrokers refer to *Registered Representative* as the industry bible. If you are selling to them, you'll probably want to be there.

There is a specialized publication for anything from Canadian chiropractors to wire wholesalers. Often there are several, even for the narrowest of niches. One of the best resources for periodicals is *Bacon's Magazine/Newspaper Directory*. Its magazine volume categorizes more than 9,500 business and consumer magazines, trade journals, and newsletters in the U.S. and Canada. Along with addresses, editors' names, phones, and fax numbers, it has brief descriptions of each publication. Call Bacon's Information at (312) 922-2400.

Newspapers.

Newspaper classifieds are excellent for reaching local markets. And newspaper classifieds are the least expensive form of advertising. Inserting a classified in a local daily or weekly general-interest paper costs no more than a business lunch. Yet newspaper classifieds pull large numbers of shoppers. They can yield huge benefits compared to the cost.

There are a wide variety of special-interest papers as well, and some of them are devoted solely to classified ads. *Hemming's Auto News* is the first classified choice for anyone advertising antique cars and vintage parts. While *Hemming's* is a national paper, there are also many local special-interest newspapers. College papers, community updates, and even industry newsletters all carry classifieds.

Newspapers provide you with the most flexibility. You can change your ad weekly or even daily. Most magazines come out either biweekly or monthly, and their advertising deadlines are usually much earlier than those for the newspapers. If your offer is especially timely, then newspapers are the way to go.

Magazines aren't as up-to-the-minute as newspapers but have the benefit of shelf life. Your ad lasts longer because people save magazines. After your first flurry of responses, you'll keep receiving inquiries from that ad for months or even years to come.

Magazine classifieds give your ads national reach. And the great variety of magazines means it is easy to reach specific groups. How else would Barbara Coole-Richman have been able to reach such a large group of parents of disabled children, except in the classifieds of *Exceptional Parent* magazine?

Online services offer the classified guerrilla rapid response to ads through return e-mail. With no printing deadlines, they're easy to update and test. You can change your ad at a moment's notice. They're convenient, too, because the addresses you collect are already in computerized form, ready for your database.

Right now, a classified ad in an online service will hit mainly upper-class males and miss most other groups. But that's changing.

Not all online services offer classifieds. But those that do can be very cost-effective for the right products and services. Business plan writer Marcia Layton's electronic classified ad on CompuServe costs only about $7.75 a week, and she has received over $10,000 in business directly from it.

Even better, some online services (like AOL) and bulletin boards will let you run your classified ads for free. You can't beat that.

TIP! Post office boxes are great for classifieds. They take less room, and people are less likely to make an addressing error.

CLASSIFIED CONSIDERATIONS

No matter what you are advertising, keep a few things in mind when you are selecting classified categories.

Look for Your Competitors' Ads.

Display advertisers never want their ads to appear next to a direct competitor's. As a classified advertiser, however you want your ad near those of competitors. If your competitors are advertising under a certain category in a certain publication over and over again, it means their ads are working. You should be there, too. The more the merrier.

Find Out What Your Customers Read.

There's nothing like an old customer or new customers just like your old ones. Clone your best customers by marketing to people like them. What publications do they read? Do they read the classifieds? Which categories? What are they shopping for? Do your best customers shop for camcorders in the Home Electronics section instead of under Cameras? Pay attention to their answers, even if they don't make sense at first.

Look for Exactly the Right Category.

New classifications appear constantly. Employment Alternatives, Air Ticket Awards. And many more you couldn't imagine if you haven't checked the classifieds lately. Microsegmentation gives a savvy guerrilla marketer a shot at hitting the market where it counts most.

You may find two classifications that sound so perfect, you can't decide between them. What to do? Run in similar sections simultaneously, of course. Check out your local newspaper's classifieds. You'll see this happening every day. A cleaning service advertises in Cleaning — Office as well as Home and Apartment Cleaning.

Double-dipping gives you a fighting chance to pick up prospects who read only one classification. And it gives you two exposures — in one day! — to people who read both. In fact, you should always be testing as many sections as possible for your ad. And if you find three tempting classifications? You know what to do.

THE FOUR PRINCIPLES OF CLASSIFIED ADVERTISING

Classified advertising is a simple concept. Yet you can build a highly sophisticated approach to it by following four basic principles:

- Test, test, and test some more.

- Be persistent.

- Follow through.

- Remember that sales count for more than responses do.

Testing.

Testing, a crucial marketing tool, is incredibly easy and effective when using classified ads. Your ads appear as soon as twenty-four hours after you place them. That lets you see quickly how well an ad is performing. Then you can revise, drop, or repeat it to yield maximum returns.

The direct response nature of classifieds makes it easy to see what's working. Put different P.O. box numbers or department codes in different versions of an ad. Have people send in a coded coupon for a free sample. Or simply collect the identifying code from each caller. Look at other people's ads and you'll quickly spot their codes. An ad in *Entrepreneur* magazine asks people to respond to Dept. ENT. Nothing could be easier.

It's usually a good idea to test just one thing at a time. Don't try new copy, a new publication, and a new category all at once. You won't know what caused the response to change. You can and should test multiple ads at the same time, however, if you code them differently.

Test different sections of the same publication. And test similar sections in different publications. Very different groups of people read the *New York Post* and the *New York Times*. The way to find out which group responds better to your ad is to test and see.

Test your ad copy. This includes the wording as well as the concept. One marketing consultant's ad says "How would you like to stop making cold calls?" A similar offer is worded "Hot leads for 7 cents each," while a third claims "500 Leads Free." More subtle differences can also affect the results. An ad that offers "Write for Brochure" may do better (or worse) than one that says "Send for Details." Experiment with the way you state your price. See if $39.99 works better than $40. Or try "Forty bucks — shipping included."

Always use headlines in boldface or all-caps, and experiment with different ones. Change the wording. Also change the way you add

 Testing is the key to the successful use of classified ads. Only change one element of your ad at a time so you can keep track of what affects your response rate. Test the length, the offer, even the day of the week you run the ad.

emphasis. Try one ad with a boldface first line that says "Free Info." A second might emphasize "ABSOLUTELY FREE!" Don't forget to try moving the punctuation marks. "New! Income Opportunity" may not pull the same as "New Income Opportunity!"

Test the action. What are you asking readers to do? You may ask them to dial an 800 number, write for a brochure, send a self-addressed stamped envelope, or possibly mail you a check. Finding out which one works will tell you a lot about your market as well as guide future ads.

Writing or, even better, calling for free useful information (not just product information) is a good action to test early on. Writing guerrilla Linda Abraham found that asking readers to call for a free pamphlet of application writing tips outdrew her other ads.

Test your benefit. Try different solutions to the reader's problem. The benefit may be a unique product or service like "The Ultimate Sawhorse" or an award-winning salsa recipe. You can try emphasizing different aspects of the benefit. Stress your salsa's rich flavor in one ad, its additive-free recipe in another.

Also test benefits such as price, terms, delivery, and guarantees. (That may be all you have if other ads offer the same products.) To advertise brand-name vitamins in *Muscle & Fitness* magazine's classifieds, a guerrilla headlined his ad, "Free Shipping! Free Handling! Free Calls! Free Technical Support!" The actual products were listed later. The response to this ad will tell clearly how important ancillary services are to this guerrilla's customers.

> Information broker and researcher Marjorie Desgrosseilliers places a classified ad in both the *Corporate Library Update* and *The Librarian's Yellow Pages* every year. Of course, the *Update* doesn't even come close to a magazine like *Newsweek* in terms of circulation, but there is no better or more targeted place for Marjorie to advertise.

Chris Beal did best with an ad offering a "Used Macintosh computer with printer" rather than a specific model. The best wording for his purpose sounds like an ad placed by an individual rather than a dealer. He's also found he needs to put a toll-free number in each ad. Testing and analysis of his responses told him that, while the Florida State University college paper yielded more calls, the Bowling Green callers were more likely to turn into buyers.

Be Persistent.

Advertise regularly and stick with it. Your ad is small and is jumbled with a bunch of other small ads. One effective way to improve your chances of being noticed is to appear there over and over. Many people do not respond to an offer the first time they see it but will on the second or third repetition.

Some publications even allot the beginning of each classified section to the longest-running ads. This is the most visible spot. (Although it's not the only good one. Many people read magazines from back to front.) It may be difficult to dethrone the first ad. If you check back issues of many magazines, you'll find that some ads have been running for ten years!

Persistence will also increase your profits by lowering the cost of each ad. Magazines and newspapers charge less per ad when you run it many times. Remember the classifieds in *Popular Science*? You can get one for only $160 a month if you run it twenty-four times.

Follow Through.

Following through is critical when you're advertising in the classifieds. *You're* asking for a response. *You* have to respond reliably.

This is more than an obligation. It's an opportunity. When you collect a response from a classified ad, you have found the most highly motivated individual in a highly motivated group. This person is interested enough in your offer to write a letter, pick up the phone, or otherwise contact you. If you have made an offer of a free sample or information, deliver it promptly.

It's not unheard of for a guerrilla offering a booklet of free tips to be deluged with thousands of requests. Check to see if you can handle the demand by testing in a limited form first. To start with, extend a less attractive offer (perhaps with a handling fee instead of free). Or try the offer in a smaller publication before rolling it out nationwide. If you can't follow through, change the offer.

Measure Results: Sales Count for More than Responses Do.

Classified ads are a marvelous way to fill your mailbox with leads. The challenge is narrowing those leads down to just the qualified ones. A guerrilla we know ran a classified campaign that generated more than 1,500 responses — and only 10 sales. It was hardly worth the cost and hassle.

As you test your classified ads, always keep the ultimate result in

 Ask for action and make it easy to respond. The reader should be compelled to do something — ideally, to place an order. Provide a toll-free phone number.

mind. Make the initial hurdle just high enough to separate the winners from the freeloaders. Test each population that responds, and try to avoid the euphoria that comes from an amazing response to an ad. Wait to celebrate until the money starts rolling in.

PLANNING AND BUDGETING FOR CLASSIFIED ADVERTISING

Money paid for a classified ad is an investment, not an expense. If that investment is to pay dividends, focusing on returns is critical. So plan ahead. Set a budget for your classified campaign. Limit your expenses to the budgeted amount. And track the returns. That will let you know whether your campaign is achieving its goals.

There's another benefit if you plan ahead. As we've already noted, your cost per insertion goes down the more times you run the ad. If you know you're going to be running an ad a couple of dozen times, you can negotiate the lower rate up front.

Setting a Budget.

Here's a hypothetical example of a guerrilla selling a small cookbook by mail from home.

FREE RECIPE! Send SASE for excerpt from new cookbook. Box 321, Dobbs Ferry, NY 10522.

This short ad can run in a wide range of publications, from specific, focused monthlies like *Chili Pepper* to more general newspapers and magazines. The publisher decided to invest $3,000 in a one-year classified ad campaign. The budget looked like this:

Magazine	Frequency	Cost per	Total
Mag. 1	monthly	$100	$1,200
Mag. 2	bimonthly	$100	$600
Mag. 3	weekly	$20	$1,040
TOTAL			$2,840

An investment of $2,840 leads to 90 ads, reaching more than 500,000 different people, generating an astounding 48 million impressions. (Of course, not every subscriber reads the classifieds. That's why the ads need to run frequently, to maximize readership.)

The book promoted by the free recipe is $20, and the cost of printing the book and putting it in a mailing envelope is $5. The cost of printing and stuffing the free sample is about 3¢. Thus, the return on each sale is $15. If the guerrilla generates just over 200 sales from the annual campaign, he breaks even.

The best part, of course, is the orders that translate into multiple sales. Even better, when the guerrilla's ready to introduce a second title, all those leads are in his computer, free and ready to go.

Budget tightly enough to control expenses. Plan loosely enough to maximize returns. If a magazine raises its rates or an ad isn't pulling enough to justify its continued insertion, don't hesitate to drop it. Plan for alternates if an ad seems marginal from the start.

Leave room to turn up the heat on a campaign that is working well. If mid-campaign results suggest you'd boost profits with more insertions, multiple categories, a toll-free phone number, or a bigger ad, give yourself the option.

DESIGNING YOUR CLASSIFIED AD

Classifieds have been around for a long time. Experience helps. We recently spotted a classified costing $300 per insertion that offered an "ingenuous" device for sale. For less than a month's advertising bill, that advertiser could have hired an expert to tell him that "ingenuous" means candid or artless. Accurate language is a major benefit you can expect from a professional copywriter. A pro knows the hot, response-building words to use. You can get solid tips about improving the look of your ad from the same source.

Does that mean you shouldn't do it yourself? Not at all. You can pick up a lot of the same knowledge a pro has by studying ads yourself, trying some ideas, and going with what works best. Check at your library for year-old issues of a publication you plan to advertise in. Compare the older classified ads to current ones. Which ones have stuck around? These must be successful ads. Borrow from them. Poring over long-lived ads will give you hints about everything from length and headline style to key phrases.

Many publications make copy consultants available at no charge to assist you with your ad's look and language. If nothing else, they'll help you avoid obvious mistakes.

Things to Include — and Some to Omit.

Certain elements should be in every ad. Others should always be left out. Still others are more variables to test. Here is a list, by no means complete, of key concerns:

- Always include a way to contact you. A classified ad without a phone number or mailing address is an exercise in futility. This could be a street address, P.O. box, toll-free phone number, fax number, or e-mail address. Remember, the purpose of this ad is to draw a direct response. Give readers easy, complete instructions.

- Use a headline. A headline in all-capital letters or boldface (or both) is your hook. It's your first and only chance to snag readers as they scan the blocks of gray in a typical classified column. Make it short, simple, and catchy. "Make Millions in Infomercials!"

- Avoid odd abbreviations and phrases. Stay away from any acronyms or obscure terms unless you're positive your audience will understand without a translator. EIK probably means nothing to you unless you live in New York City. There, guerrilla real estate brokers can safely use it to indicate an Eat-In Kitchen. For a national classified, or one you plan to run in many places, stick to everyday language.

- Use words like "Free" and "New" and "Guaranteed." Most classifieds use one of these words. Some use all three. They work. Probably the most used classified phrase of all time is "Call or write for our FREE brochure." It may not be original, but it's ageless magic for guerrilla marketers.

- Describe benefits. The features of your product or service are important. "Incredible New Money-Making Breakthrough!" is a feature. "You can make up to $25,000 a month" is a benefit. Benefits are what sell.

Don't write copy that sounds different just for the sake of being different. While you don't want to steal other ads outright, remember that millions of guerrillas have spent years honing this medium. Take from the best ads, press the proven hot buttons, and then test, test, test.

Let the offer determine the copy. An ad selling herbs to vegetarians in a Buddhist newsletter will have a different tone than one urging gam-

 TIP! "Free" is a very powerful word, but if you use it in your classified ad, be prepared to handle the response. One guerrilla offered a free brochure in his ad and had to mail out over 1,500 brochures at a cost of $1 each.

blers to send for free tips on winning poker. Imagine how you would present this offer to a prospect in person. Then write the ad as if you were speaking directly to the prospect.

Learn the rules concerning boldface and capital letters. Many publications restrain the use of highlighted type. For instance, you may not be able to set more than one line in black boldface. Since you won't see your ad before it appears, it's important to know the rules before you send it in.

Rent a P.O. box. It costs a nominal sum and may save your ad budget sizable amounts. You pay for each line of type in a classified. And "P.O. Box 111" is shorter than a typical street address. Especially if you live on a street with a long name, consider using a P.O. box for your classified mail drop.

Use a post office in another town. If you live in Dalworthington Gardens, Texas, you might rent a box at the post office in nearby Irving. It's shorter and therefore cheaper. Not to mention that since the Dallas Cowboys play their home games in Irving, it's familiar to many people.

Try a classified display ad. These are about a quarter of the price of display ads and may pull much better. They still appear in the classified section, but they have borders around them and use larger, darker type than the regular ads. This hybrid is worth looking into if you're not satisfied with your classified response.

Don't be afraid to test a long ad. If you have a unique product that requires some explanation, it's a false economy to keep your ad as short as possible. Use short words and short concepts. But don't leave out important features or benefits. The cost of your ad is measured only in terms of the response it generates. If spending a few more dollars for a few more lines can increase sales, it's worth it.

Typical classifieds are two to four lines long. Occasionally you see one that is fifteen or even twenty lines long. Such an eye catcher can convey far more than the telegram-style classified. If your concept needs it, or lackluster results have you looking for new ideas, try the long classified.

Leave something out. You're trying to generate a response, not necessarily a sale. So leave something out that the customer would need to make a buying decision. It could be the price, location, or exact product you're offering. An interested reader will contact you for details. Computer shoppers who see Chris Beal's $500 computer ad are sure to wonder why the price is so low. When they call to find out, his ad is halfway to working. Give enough information to generate interest. Leave enough out to spur action. That's what classified ads are all about.

9 NETWORKING
GENERATING BUSINESS THROUGH PERSONAL CONTACT

WHEN ALLEN HARPHAM STARTED HIS home-based computer consulting firm, his first call wasn't to a prospect. It was to another computer consultant. His second call wasn't to a prospect. It was to another consultant. His third call? His old boss. Then the Chamber of Commerce.

By calling all these people and organizations to touch base and let them know what he was up to, Allen was building a marketing network. Does it work? Here's what happened to him:

- Other computer consultants became his major source of business. They refer overflow work from their own, better-established businesses.

- His former employer became one of his biggest clients.

- The Chamber of Commerce appointed Allen to its new Technology Committee. This volunteer position has yielded lots of invaluable exposure to other businesses and to the media.

Many guerrillas will tell you that one of the most effective ways to make a business grow is through networking. And why not? As a home-based business owner, you can get out and meet your prospects in person. Large corporations have a hard time matching that level of personal contact.

TWO PILLARS OF NETWORKING

As you begin to network, keep two things in mind: trust and balance. You already know that a lack of trust leads to lost sales. The personal contacts and referrals that come from networking can overcome fear and build trust. But if you are too aggressive when you network, you break down trust rather than build it up.

The expensive way to build trust is through advertisements ("You can trust your car to the man who wears the star"). But customers don't naturally trust corporations, slogans, or organizations. They trust people.

Home-based computer equipment importer Svante Rodegard says lack of trust is the biggest complaint European business people have about Americans. How does he overcome this barrier? By informally networking — creating a relationship before he tries to make the sale.

Svante is Swedish, which gives him an advantage in the Swedish marketplace. He can easily build relationships with Swedish business people because he speaks their language and can relate to their culture. He networks by phone with his customers in Sweden all the time, calling them just to chat about his homeland or find out how their families are doing. His customers know that he cares about them and that he is personally available to meet their needs. That is critical for any guerrilla trying to build trust. When you are doing business from thousands of miles away, it's even more so.

Networking is potentially an around-the-clock activity. Any contact with anyone can conceivably be an opportunity to network. But, depending on your profession, you can go too far.

For example, we know an insurance salesman who gets into crowded elevators, announces "Thank you all for coming to this meeting," and begins handing out business cards.

He's too in-your-face to be networking. It's group prospecting. Imagine a similar technique used by a plastic surgeon or a high-class art appraiser. If the surgeon kept walking up to people at cocktail parties, pointing out facial features that he could improve, his networking technique would backfire. Same thing with the art appraiser. If she went to parties and constantly went around the room announcing the value of everything in it...Well, you get the idea.

If networking is high pressure instead of low key, if it is transparent-

 TIP! You're not the only one who wants to network. Don't be shy about introducing yourself — the person you're meeting probably wants to make contact with you as well.

ly an attempt to generate sales rather than develop relationships, it won't be nearly as successful.

How do you find a balance? Don't approach each prospect as an opportunity to make a sale. Instead, realize that all long-term relationships are reciprocal. If you help strangers, they're far more likely to want to work with you in the future.

The Golden Rule of Networking: You can get anything in life if you just help enough other people get what they want.

Join a committee — not to meet people, but to improve the neighborhood. Refer a hard-working neighbor to a fast-growing business and you've made two friends by helping both. Clip articles and mail them to people

> One of your best networking sources is your competition. That may seem odd, but imagine owning a desktop publishing business that specializes in corporate identity packages. A client asks you to design an annual report during your busy season. You really don't have the time or the expertise to do the job right, but you don't want to turn down the business. Refer the client to the company across town that specializes in annual reports. Your client will appreciate your honesty and the referral, and you can be sure that the next time your competitor is overloaded, she will send some business your way.

who might be interested. You've done a service, even if it only took a few minutes and a stamp.

Chris Locke is a true electronic guerrilla. Over the last two years, he's sent more than 7,000 e-mail notes. Most of the time, he's offering to help. He helps people discover data, make contacts, get the inside scoop on technology. So far, he's contributed to three of our books. And he rarely tries to sell anything or ask a favor. But when Chris does need a consulting job or an introduction to a potential client or even an opinion, you can bet he'll get what he asks for. Why? Because his contacts are frequent and regular. That builds familiarity and trust. And his contacts are informal, simple e-mail notes asking if there's any way he can help. That keeps things relaxed. And relaxed people are more willing to trust. He discusses almost everything but his business, except on a casual level. This guerrilla is building a genuine relationship with his hundreds of "friends" by staying in touch.

Sound like a lot of work? Say Chris spends thirty minutes a day networking. In that time, he is able to do more than direct mail, advertising, and trade shows exhibits could ever deliver for him. When we last spoke to Chris, he had just landed a plum job for a major phone company. His networking got him noticed, got him trusted — got him the job.

When you're networking, don't wait for someone to help you. Do something for the other person first. Do it selflessly and for a long period of time. It will pay off. People will know if you're itching to have the relationship pay off. Don't sabotage yourself. Do for others because you can and you want to, not because a sale will result tomorrow.

WHAT NETWORKING CAN DO FOR YOU

Selling without selling, helping without demanding anything in return — networking so far sounds like a surefire way to go broke. But there are solid reasons that you should network, and real benefits in the end.

Establish Your Reputation in the Community.

Appearing as a speaker, teaching a seminar, participating in local benefits and nonprofit groups, and just showing up for meetings can all increase people's trust in you.

Realize that community is not necessarily geographical. Your community is your industry or your market, not where you live. Delores Ruzicka lives in Nebraska, but her community is the national and international community of craft designers.

Position Yourself as an Expert.

When you're introduced as a luncheon speaker, identified as a donor of goods or services, or elected as an organization's officer, the label "expert" naturally comes up. The real beauty is you don't even have to apply the label yourself. The people you're networking with will do it for you.

Repetition Is Rarely Overdone in Marketing.

When people see you over and over again, they remember you. You do it with your advertisements and direct mail pieces, right? Why not do the same with your own voice and face?

Home-based designer David Tisdale strives to keep his face in front of his prospects as much as possible. He stresses that he doesn't do it in an irritating, pushy way. "Rather," he says, "it comes from the realization that the more people hear or read about me, or see me in person, the more likely they'll think of me first when a project comes along."

 TIP! Networking secret: do for others before you ask them to do for you. Offer help, advice, news clippings, and new business referrals to as many people as you can. Soon, your good work will be returned in kind.

THREE CORE CONCEPTS

Networking isn't as easy as it sounds. Most people find it a little tricky at first. They don't know how to get started, or they're nervous about appearing to be gladhanding or insincere. Some tips:

Be Patient.

Networking on a deadline rarely works. Be prepared to invest at least six months of steady effort before you start seeing the results of your work.

Donna Lewein says it has taken a year and a half of networking to pay off for the Scribe Shop. When she and her husband, Scott, moved their home-based business from Washington, D.C., to Oregon, Wisconsin, they hit the networking ground running. Among their networking initiatives:

- Donna joined a group of women entrepreneurs.

- The Leweins joined a barter association.

- They belong to their Chamber of Commerce.

- The couple gave discount design services to a local nonprofit organization that helps people with disabilities, prisoners, and the economically disadvantaged prepare for the workplace.

- They joined the Madison Area Business Consultants organization.

Make no mistake: the Leweins are not the kind of members who pay their dues but never show their faces. When the Chamber of Commerce sponsored a business card exchange day, they were there. The same group's small business awards breakfast was also on their schedule.

It took eighteen months of attending the different groups' monthly meetings, but they are beginning to get some good jobs out of the connections they have made. In fact, Donna claims that networking has been by far the most successful marketing tool for their business.

The Leweins recognize that persistence is the key to building a home business. They set goals and stick with them. They networked in the same places for months before they saw any return. By building relationships, they have been able to build a business, one contact at a time.

Follow Up.

Don't expect to meet someone at a networking function, have them express interest in your service, and call you the next day with an order. Networking is just the first step in the relationship.

Your follow-up doesn't necessarily involve trying to sell right away. If you meet someone and then see something in the paper you think might interest him, clip it and send it. E-mail him about a book he might enjoy. Call and ask how the project he told you about turned out.

Following up on a networking contact is an excellent opportunity for you to employ your other guerrilla marketing tools, such as:

- Direct mail. Snagging a business card from a networking contact gives you everything you need to address a direct mail letter. And the conversation you engaged in while collecting the card should give you plenty of information to add a clutter-busting personal note.

- Telephone. Few things can increase the likelihood your call will be accepted and listened to more than beginning with: "Hi, we met at the breakfast last week, and I was just…"

- Newsletter. You've shown a networking contact your informal, personal side at a face-to-face meeting. Now put your best marketing foot forward by following up with a newsletter that tells about your business, offers tips, and encourages a response in polished, professional prose.

- Brochure or media kit. Never try to tell people you've just met as much about your business as they could learn from a brochure. You'll most likely bore them. Concentrate on asking them questions when you're face to face. Perhaps pique their curiosity about your business by being a little reticent. Then satisfy it by mailing them a full brochure or media kit.

- E-mail. The beauty of e-mail is its speed. It's easy to send e-mail to a contact before he or she even returns to the office from your meeting. What better way to reinforce that initial impression than with a one-two communications punch?

Dallas marketing consultant Kevin Knight realized the potential of a single, carefully followed-up networking opportunity for his home-based business. After giving a speech on marketing communications to a group of executives, he handed out bound copies of articles reinforcing his points. Within a few days, each attendant got a letter thanking him or her for listening, reiterating a few tips, and offering to help at any time. Within a year, he had cultivated six figures' worth of sales from

 Always give contacts two business cards. When they point out the extra, ask them to pass one on to a friend — and offer to do the same for the person you're talking to.

people he met through that one engagement.

Leverage Your Marketing Efforts.

Be picky. It's easy to misdirect your energy and spend too much time with contacts that will never turn into sales or even good referrals. It's important that all the networking you do counts. Target your contacts. Look for people who have a lot of influence with and access to your market. And make sure your appearance at a networking function is high profile.

According to a story in *Home Office Computing*, Susan RoAne, a home-based speaker and author, found that one of the best ways to increase her business was to start an informal networking group. The first thing she did was to invite her stockbroker, accountant, and lawyer to dinner. The group grew from there and is now a forum for all types of business people to get together, exchange ideas, and cooperate on projects.

Stand out at a meeting by offering to help in some way. The ideal situation is to be a featured speaker. If that job's taken, ask if you can introduce the speaker or chair a panel. Maybe your company can sponsor a refreshment break or provide free audio cassettes of the speech to participants.

Crafts business owner Donna Heidler believes that she is always three people away from the person she wants to talk to. Here's how she made the hop, skip, and jump to one key contact.

A retail needlework shop owner (#1) introduced her to a published crochet designer (#2), who exposed her to the Society of Craft Designers, where, after joining, she met an editor (#3) who bought a design to feature in a magazine. Her lesson: the importance of talking to everyone about her business.

TRADE SHOWS

Many trade shows seem to be dominated by huge displays set up by giant corporations. But notice all the guerrillas standing around the glitzy booths — they're networking, and probably doing more combined business than the behemoths.

Just because you're not dumping a bundle into a booth is no reason

 TIP! Everyone in America is six handshakes away from everyone else. So, even if you don't know your biggest prospect personally, you probably know someone, who knows someone, who does.

to be casual about networking at a trade show. Before you pin on your name badge, develop a written three-pronged strategy. Decide:

1. What you're after. It could be information about the competition, details of problems potential customers are having, or industry news. Whatever you seek, set a goal so you don't get sidetracked.

2. What you'll offer. Don't expect something for nothing. Plan to lure network opportunities with valuable information, free samples — even just a chance to share a table at the end of a foot-tiring day.

3. Whom you're after. Pick the groups with whom you'll network. If you are there to sell, for instance, seek out buyers and avoid other vendors. This will help you decide quickly which meeting invitations to accept. Trade shows can be overwhelming. Stay focused on your goals.

Many trade show visitors erect an invisible wall around themselves. They act as if they're walking through a crowded street in a city, avoiding eye contact and rushing from place to place. While these people may visit a lot of booths, they're missing the highlight of the show — an opportunity to meet valuable contacts on neutral ground.

As a guerrilla, you need to break through this wall. Most trade shows give attendees a big name tag. Take advantage of it. When waiting in line (there are always lines!), call your fellow line-standers by name. Ask them about their companies. Find out why they came to the show. Figure out if you know anyone in common.

Turn this "chance" contact into an opportunity to exchange cards. Try to figure out a referral you can give your new friend. Do you know a company or service that can help her business? Ask for advice with your problems. You'll probably get some worthwhile wisdom, and you're also building a relationship.

Delores Ruzicka built a business doing what she loves (crafting ceramics, arranging flowers, woodworking, selling craft supplies, and more) largely on the strength of some persistent, well-targeted networking. She goes to hundreds of craft shows a year — and sponsors three shows of her own.

A member of the Society of Craft Designers, Delores attends the annual convention where publishers, editors, manufacturers, and

TIP! Print some useful information on the back of your business card (metric conversion, common phone numbers, etc.). Then you can give out cards freely, without worrying about overstepping the bounds of a social occasion.

designers all get together. That is where she sells a lot of her designs to craft magazines. In fact, her Cinnamon Street line of cards, rubber stamps, iron-ons, and wrapping paper was born of a contact made at a convention.

ASSOCIATIONS AND PROFESSIONAL ORGANIZATIONS

Many groups don't hold conventions but still provide prime networking opportunities. These include social clubs, country clubs, service clubs, and health clubs, as well as the more obvious trade groups and associations.

Even though many members of an association are competitors, you'll be surprised at how willing people are to share secrets, exchange customers, and generally be helpful. Nobody wants to be a competitive boor.

Mollie Wakeman, who runs a busy music teaching studio in her home in California, has never found it necessary to advertise for students. In fact, she's always had a lengthy waiting list. What's her secret?

After joining a music teachers association, Mollie quickly learned the benefits of networking with the competition. Once she acquainted the other members with her special skills and background, teachers with jammed schedules or a lack of expertise in certain areas began to refer students to her. Of course, she did the same for them.

Once you belong to an association, its membership list becomes a ticket to year-round networking. Call a different member every week just to chat. You'll be surprised at how quickly you can build a network.

If there is no suitable local organization for you to join, how about starting one?

Terry Wohlers started the Rapid Prototyping Association with thirteen other industry members because he felt there was a need for people to share information. The RPA's number one objective was to provide something that the industry needed. So far, about 1,200 other people have agreed with him and become members.

Maybe there's already a pretty good association in your industry, but

TIP! When attending any networking event, always carry a stack of business cards and a pen or pencil. Write a note to yourself on the back of any business cards you collect to remind yourself what you talked about. It can be frustrating to collect cards from others and not be able to remember them.

it's too large or too diffuse for your purposes. You can raise your profile within that organization by becoming more involved. Join a special-interest committee. Your networking circle will immediately become tighter, and you'll enjoy many more networking benefits.

SPEAKING ENGAGEMENTS

When people speak in public, they are perceived as experts in their field. A good way to get your business off the ground or to gain new contacts is to offer your services as a speaker to local organizations, businesses, and even schools. In the beginning, you will probably have to speak for free, but as your reputation grows, you may be able to charge a fee.

Motivational speaker Zig Ziglar says he gave more than 3,000 free speeches before getting paid. But along the way, he spoke to hundreds of thousands of people — people who now know and trust him. Those same people eventually built the base for his business.

Teach a class or give a seminar. When you provide education, you're giving people something of great value — and they appreciate it. Not sure how to get started? Sign up to attend a seminar. Find out who organized it. Ask to be a speaker at the next one.

The Learning Annex is a nationwide chain of continuing education schools. They offer inexpensive courses in everything from massage to cooking to accounting. While Learning Annex teachers don't get paid a lot of cash, they make thousands in useful contacts.

Guerrilla Marcia Layton gives frequent one-shot seminars on starting a business and writing business plans. Isn't she just telling people how to get along without her? Nope. A single presentation to the Rochester Engineering Society turned into three hot leads.

You get two marketing bangs per buck when you teach a regular class, notes home-based management consultant Sue Inches, who serves on the adjunct faculty of two Maine colleges. First, you get direct contact with the members of your class. Second, you are listed by name and specialty in a printed course catalog, which gets a much wider distribution.

When you teach a class or give a speech, bring along plenty of business cards. Even better, hand each student a printed syllabus on your letterhead. It makes your course more effective and makes it easy for a student to find you later.

COMMUNITY INVOLVEMENT

Getting involved in everything from neighborhood groups to political parties can produce valuable contacts, credentials, and referrals. There's some residual value as well. It will make you feel good.

Home-based marketing consultant Hank Walshak did more than join the Pittsburgh High Technology Council and the Rotary club when he began his networking efforts. He also started working pro bono for these organizations. Hank volunteered to publicize a campaign his Rotary club started to get children vaccinated. In the process, he got some publicity of his own — doing well while doing good.

This is one area where self-serving networking will definitely get you in trouble. People are offended when a company or individual appears to be using a charitable event for personal gain. If you can't contribute without the hope of getting rewarded, better focus on another form of networking.

When Roslyn Goldman started an art appraisal and consulting service out of her home in 1985, she had no clients. Networking was the answer. She took an active role in the regional and national arts community. She headed a controversial art project at the local airport, organized an extensive list of speaking engagements about public art, and developed several programs for art groups, museums, libraries, and other organizations. These activities helped to establish Roslyn as a serious promoter of the arts and a reputable appraiser. Her business, as well as her network of friends, colleagues, and clients, has continued to grow ever since.

ONLINE NETWORKING

On commercial online services like CompuServe and America Online, you'll find decision-makers. And the segmented nature of the services makes it easy to find the people in your industry. They are all there, just waiting for you to contribute your ideas on bulletin boards, in chat rooms, and in libraries.

A guerrilla in Kentucky built a $6 million a year software distribution business using only the Internet for marketing. For six months, all he did was answer technical questions for people online. He never asked for anything in return — he just managed to be helpful to almost everyone who crossed his path.

When he started his software distribution business, where did he find his core audience? Online, of course. In gratitude for all the help he'd given, literally thousands of people became his customers. He'd built trust by doing for others without reward, and he was rewarded for it in the end.

Marcia Layton spreads word of her business plan writing skills through the business forum on CompuServe. Although she can't shake hands and pass out business cards from a computer terminal, she effectively networks by responding to requests for information and advice. She gives people tips on writing plans and on starting businesses and always ends the message by telling people what she does. The combination of friendly assistance and professional identification has built Marcia a lot of online credibility.

You can do more than offer friendly advice online. You even have a chance to give "speeches." Most online services allow you to post files containing essays or even books. If you are a marketing consultant, write an article filled with marketing tips and post it in the library of the marketing forum on CompuServe. At the end of the article, mention who you are, what you do, and where you can be reached. People who download the article, like what you have to say, and need some specialized marketing help are likely to call you for some advice.

The best rule of thumb for succeeding online is to go slow and watch what other folks are doing. There's no room for a hard sell here. You've got to build trust slowly, over time.

STAYING IN TOUCH

Richard Cassell is a voice-over specialist in New York. Voice-over work is lucrative (hundreds of dollars an hour) but hard to find.

So Richard spends ten minutes a day making calls to a list of people he's worked with. In ten minutes he can make 10 calls. That means he reaches more than 200 people a month. If you've ever used him, odds are you'll hear from Richard about once every two months.

The message is short and simple: "Hi, it's Richard Cassell, just checking in..."

Every two months he mails each person on his list a simple postcard. Sometimes he announces his newest job; sometimes he includes a list of

 TIP! Networking takes time. Don't expect to sign up any new accounts at the first Chamber of Commerce meeting you attend. The goal is to build trust over time. Plan to devote at least six months of your time to any networking organization before you see any results in the form of new customers.

tips for using professional voice-over in different industries. The point is to remind people he's there and eager to work for them.

You can bet that if any of his four hundred contacts need a radio commercial or other voice-over work, they'll remember Richard.

Think for a minute about all the similar things you can do to stay in touch with people. You'd be surprised at what you can come up with in the way of guerrilla networking opportunities. Some suggestions:

 If you have recently left the corporate world to start a home-based business, one of your best networking sources could be a former employer. Glen Stockton, a home-based graphic designer in Croton, N.Y., left a large design firm in New York City to go it alone. Rather than burn his bridges, he stayed in touch with his former employer who, in fact, became his first big client. Since then, the design executive has filled Glen's testimonial notebook and has sent several new clients his way.

- Write notes to colleagues every day. When was the last time you got a friendly note just saying "hi" from a colleague? We'll bet you remember it because it's so rare. You can cut through the networking clutter by sending your own notes out regularly to people you know or would like to know.

- Clip articles about people or their companies and mail them along with a short note.

- Refer business and leads to other people. Networking, more than most marketing efforts, is a two-way street. Contributing your share will generate goodwill and referrals back to you.

- Start an e-mail mailing list to keep in touch. It's easy and inexpensive to set up an electronic mailing list that you can use to update contacts for your business. Be sure to seek out their messages, too!

- Start a newsletter. By encouraging reader responses, a newsletter can be a great networking tool. Show you're listening by providing answers in your newsletter to the problems you hear your customers talking about.

TIP! Online services are a great place to network. Start hanging around in forums where people discuss subjects pertaining to your business. Offer advice and share ideas. You can meet hundreds of highly qualified leads there without ever leaving your desk.

- Take advantage of holidays, anniversaries, and other events as reasons to send a card or note or to call contacts. Don't limit yourself to the traditional year-end holiday card. You'll get lost in the clutter. Joe Girard, the greatest car salesman who ever lived, sent every person who'd ever bought a car from him a greeting card every month. Twelve times a year you'd hear from Joe. Mother's Day. Labor Day. Even Thanksgiving. When it was time to buy a new car, there was little doubt you'd at least give Joe a chance at your business.

10 TELEPHONE
A POWERFUL HOME-BASED GUERRILLA TOOL

WHAT IF THERE WAS A WAY YOU COULD REACH almost any prospect, anywhere in the world, for less than a dollar? A technology that would offer instant communication to discover exactly what your customer was thinking, a technology in which your company's size and marketing budget were irrelevant?

The telephone can give you the edge your business needs. But only if you use it wisely. The most important thing you can do on the phone is ask questions. Ask about your clients' needs, their family, their business, and any other topic they want to talk about. Use the telephone to establish personal, individual connections between you and your customers.

Because the telephone is such a powerful personal guerrilla weapon, it's also dangerous. Every time you call an individual you are an interruption and uninvited. This potential etiquette disaster was first addressed by Thomas Edison.

After Alexander Graham Bell invented the phone, he had trouble getting people to use it. One big problem was that members of polite society didn't go barging in on other people — there was no simple way to initiate a conversation. There wasn't even a word or phrase to get them started.

Bell wanted people to pick up the phone and say "ahoy." He figured that if it was good enough for sailors, it would also work well on the phone.

Fortunately, Edison stepped in and substituted "hello." Now there was a way to answer a call from a stranger and set a gracious tone.

Since that first hello, the telephone has walked a fine line between the benefits of immediate communication and the pitfalls of interrupting people. Astute guerrillas know how to use the phone to get what they need from prospects and customers without being obnoxious.

Businesses spend over $70 billion a year on telemarketing. As a marketing expenditure, it's bigger than television ads, bigger than newspaper ads, bigger than direct mail — bigger than anything else.

Yet telemarketing is the perfect tool for the small business. It's the great equalizer. As a home-based guerrilla, you can make the calls or answer the callers yourself. Unlike the big guys, you'll be able to offer your prospects access to a fully informed decision-maker — you.

Just like direct mail, though, you won't be effective using this technique the same way the big guys do. Large telemarketers live and die by increasing their response rate by .5%. They call thousands of names, bothering people who have no desire to hear about their product, all in the hope of making a few sales. Guerrillas want nothing of this. They want to focus on their targets like a laser beam, generating a hit rate that would make an ordinary telemarketer swoon.

> When making a sales call, try to make sure you are talking to the decision-maker before launching into your pitch. Dawn Orford, a home-based trade show consultant, starts by calling the company and asking for the name of the person who decides whether or not the company participates in trade shows. Then she tries to reach that person directly. If she can't, she sends a letter.

Telephone marketing is not as personal as a face-to-face sales call but it's far more time- and cost-efficient. The typical personal sales call costs a company about $300 in expenses and manpower. In many cases, a phone call can accomplish the same goals.

Telemarketing comes in two varieties: outgoing and incoming. Incoming telemarketing requires the prospect to call you. Outgoing telemarketing requires you to call the prospects.

Incoming telemarketing involves people who respond to the advertisements, mail, or other marketing methods you've used to reach them. The good news is that since the prospects are calling you, you don't have to worry about contacting the right people or reaching them at a bad time. The bad news is that getting someone to pick up the phone and call you isn't always easy.

Successful guerrillas know that a successful incoming telemarketing

TIP! Record yourself on the phone. You'll be amazed at how you sound. By reviewing your pitch, you can make it infinitely better.

program is only the tip of a huge iceberg. Letters, ads, brochures, and business cards must all work together to get the prospect to call you.

FIVE TIPS FOR GENERATING INCOMING CALLS

1. Make It Easy.

Toll-free 800 numbers are now available from all the major long-distance companies. They can cost as little as $20 a month and can be installed on a residential phone line.

A toll-free number gives you instant credibility. It establishes a sense of security and longevity that you can't duplicate in any other way. Even a strictly local business — plumbing — can benefit from a toll-free number.

2. Consider a Number That Spells Something.

Marjorie Desgrosseillier's number for her home-based AccuSearch Information Services is 1-800-201-INFO. Numbers that spell something work best if you're able to distribute the number in print. People often think that they'll remember your number if it spells a word, but they forget quickly.

3. Make Your Number a Fixture.

Offer stickers, Rolodex cards, refrigerator magnets, desk ornaments — anything that makes it easy for someone to find your number when they need it. A car repair shop had a joint venture with a car wash. In exchange for recommending the car wash to every customer, the repair shop got a small sticker with its phone number placed on the windshield of every car going through the car wash. You can be sure that anyone needing repair would have no trouble finding the number.

4. Offer a Benefit.

It's easy to put off calling someone — but harder if calling before tomorrow means a free gift.

TIP! Following up direct mail letters with phone calls increases the response rate by anywhere from 6% to 22%.

5. Repeat Yourself.

People may not respond the first, second, third, or even the fourth time they see your ad and number. But sooner or later you'll hear from them. Persist.

WHOM TO TARGET AND HOW

Most home-based businesses have no desire to deal with the general public. Instead, they're looking for targeted audiences for their specific services. You can increase the success of your incoming telemarketing by making sure you target and reach the right audience.

Teri's Typing Service decided that addressing envelopes would be a great way to grow. By focusing on businesses that no longer had typewriters (just laser printers), Teri decided that she could create a profitable niche.

But how could she find businesses that needed a lot of envelopes addressed? She decided to create a business card–size flyer. It read:

Teri's Typing Service
We Specialize in Envelopes
From 10 to 10,000, professionally hand-typed
Guaranteed Quality
(800) 555-2300

She printed 5,000 cards for less than $200. Once she had a vehicle, the challenge was to reach businesses that needed her. This called for a little more creativity (and shoe leather). She distributed the card in a number of places.

- She posted them on the bulletin boards at every post office in the county.

- She placed one on the cash register at every copy shop in the county.

- She arranged to have her card included in every job a local envelope printer sent out. (Every time he printed envelopes for anyone, he enclosed her card. In exchange, she did free typing for the printer.)

 TIP! The Golden Rule of Telephone Selling: Never call someone without a referral. If you can't tell the caller the name of a mutual friend, acquaintance, or organization, don't bother calling.

BE PREPARED WHEN THE PHONE RINGS

After the phone rings, you've got to make all your effort pay off. An astute guerrilla will use a script and a strategy — not just wing it.

Home-based doll designer Donna Hawley uses a variety of marketing tools — brochures, mail order ads, networking, and more — to initiate relationships with prospects. She relies heavily on the telephone to follow up and build on those relationships.

When manufacturers, retailers, or consumers call, Donna goes beyond just answering their questions. She gets personal, asking callers where they are from and chatting with them about their interests.

Along the way, she gathers information, such as what types of stores are nearby and whether there is an outlet for her products. If they recommend a good retail outlet that might carry her wares, she gives them something for free or a discount on their order.

Donna's phone marketing style puts her in a different galaxy from the big-name doll companies. Mattel Inc. may have Barbie, but the chairperson of the company isn't going to schmooze with customers about where they shop. Donna is taking this difference and making the most of it through the telephone.

Your company's image is displayed the moment you answer the phone. Surprisingly, most companies do an awful job of introducing themselves by phone. Find out for yourself. Open the Yellow Pages and dial any number you find. When the phone is answered, listen carefully to what you hear.

- Can you figure out whom you've called?

- Are you encouraged by a clear, friendly voice?

- Do you feel as though you've interrupted an important meeting?

What you'll learn is that most businesses have no idea how to answer the phone. Here are four general elements to include in your own ideas:

1. Consistency. Always answer your phone the same way. This consistency gives callers a comfortable feeling. Train yourself and your employees in the exact wording and voice inflection to use.

2. Identification. Name your business clearly in your standard greeting:

 TIP! Resist the temptation to interrupt your prospect in midsentence to refute a point he has made. Hear him out and then address everything all at once.

"This is Guild Graphics." Adding the answerer's name helps put things on a personal basis: "Eileen speaking."

3. Benefits. Include a brief benefit in your greeting: "Barton's Limo, all cars smoke-free." Keep your benefit brief. You don't want to waste a caller's time, especially repeat callers, who have heard the greeting before.

4. Friendliness. Make your standard greeting friendly: "Season's greetings from Catering Creations." The telephone can be an impersonal tool if you don't work to maintain a relaxed air.

Our favorite guerrilla when it comes to the telephone is the Zig Ziglar Corporation. Zig writes books and gives speeches on motivation, and his staff answers the phone in just a few words but certainly makes an impact. It's worth a call: (214) 383-3221.

BE GOAL-ORIENTED ON THE PHONE

While the image you present to callers is important, image isn't everything. A script can help you stay on track. Here are some of the things you should try to accomplish while you are on the phone with a prospect.

Gather Information.

When dealing with a new prospect on the phone, always start the conversation by writing down the caller's name and phone number ("in case we get disconnected"). This will make it easier to call people by name and also ensure that you never lose a lead.

Once you've got the name and phone number, you should probably follow a script for determining how you can best help the caller. Ask a lot of questions. Not just, "What can I do for you today?" Asking increasingly detailed questions about a caller's problem shows you are interested and knowledgeable. The more you know about the problem, the better you can help.

Continue the Relationship.

Depending on your business, you'll either want to set up a personal

 TIP! If you are having trouble getting through a gatekeeper, try calling your prospect at odd hours. Call before or after typical business hours or during lunchtime, when gatekeepers are out and people tend to answer their own phones.

meeting, send out a brochure, or try to close the sale right there. Have well-rehearsed scripts ready to deal with whichever approach is most appropriate. Some key points to remember:

Move gradually up to a commitment. Abruptly asking for an order will work a small percentage of the time. You'll have better success by making a carefully planned series of points leading to the inevitable decision to buy from you. Establish a need for your product or service. Show why you're different from the competition. Offer something extra. Then go for the commitment.

Don't ask questions that can be answered with a "no." Instead, try to ask questions that you know will get a "yes" or offer choices, such as, "Would you like this better in red or blue?"

Don't stop if you're on a roll. If you ask for an order or appointment and get one, go for more. Ask new customers if they'd like an accessory for that product they just bought — it's on sale this week. If you get an appointment for a sales presentation, suggest that a short visit to one of your existing clients might also be instructive. If someone has said yes once, they're likely to say it again.

If you can't help the caller, don't hesitate to make a referral to a competitor who can. People will never believe you if you tell them you're not aware of anyone else who has the solution. You've done nothing but lose a customer for life. By cheerfully sacrificing a potential sale to help solve their problem, you'll gain credibility and generate goodwill that will soon come back to you.

Don't leave the next step up to the prospect. If you're sending out a brochure, make it clear in your beautifully typed and personalized cover letter that you will call them in ten days to answer any other questions they may have. If you decide to set up a meeting, don't end the call without a specific time to meet or the name of a secretary you can call to book the time.

TECHNOLOGY COUNTS

One thing that's especially important to home-based guerrillas is a hold button. Make sure your phone has one. Isn't it amazing how many home-based business folks continue to answer the phone with screaming babies, barking dogs, and other noises in the background? It doesn't sound very professional.

On the other hand, think twice about using call waiting. For an informal business, this is a low-cost way to reduce busy signals. But for not much more money, you can install a second line with rollover. This will direct all calls for the first line to a second phone if the first is busy. You'll be able to put people on hold or let an answering machine pick up.

A second option is call answering. This service is provided by the telephone company for a few dollars a month. It is a rudimentary voice-mail service that essentially acts like an answering machine, but has one important difference: nobody ever gets a busy signal. A regular answering machine, even one hooked up to a two-line rollover, can't guarantee that. In these days of nearly universal voice-mail, many people will not redial once they get a busy signal.

> When making a sales call, Hank Walshak of Walshak Communications, a home-based marketing and consulting firm, makes a point of asking if he has called at a good time. Hank has found that his politeness goes a long way. If you ask people for permission to talk to them for a few minutes, they will be much more receptive. Of course, if it's not a good time, he tries to make an appointment to call at a better time.

If you frequently put people on hold, investigate the opportunity to use the new low-cost music-on-hold and tape-on-hold systems. These allow you to make the wait more tolerable or, even better, to create a taped announcement that outlines all the services your company offers.

Do the same with your outgoing answering message. Instead of apologizing for the lack of a receptionist, take advantage of your answering machine as a marketing tool. Instead of a ten-second message, use thirty seconds and give the caller some added benefit or message. Here are some suggestions:

- Mention a recent article on your company or an ad you've recently run: "As you may have read in Sunday's *New York Times*, we are now offering..."

- Talk about a special event that is coming up in which you are participating: "Come see us at the Worldwide trade show next month."

- Announce a contest you are running: "Be sure to ask us for information on our sweepstakes. You have only two more weeks to enter."

TIP! Don't feel as though every time you pick up the phone, you have to sell something. Call one of your existing customers just to thank them for their recent business. Make 2 thank-you calls a day, and you'll reach more than 400 people a year.

- Tell a success story. If you managed to save a client 70% on a telephone bill, say so.

- Offer a piece of business information the caller might find useful: "According to *Nation's Business* magazine, you can save up to 30% on your Federal Express bill by renegotiating with the company."

Ilise Benun, who publishes the newsletter "The Art of Self-Promotion," says that you should include the following items in your answering machine message to turn it into a marketing tool:

1. A short blurb about the services and products you offer.

2. Your fax number.

3. Announcements and upcoming events.

4. Special discounts you are offering.

Speaking of answering machines, here's another way to improve your business. Hire a local actor or actress to record your message. The sound quality and delivery will make it much more likely that people will hang up with a good impression.

OUTSTANDING OUTBOUND TELEMARKETING

When most people think of telemarketing, they think of traditional outbound telemarketing: leagues of ill-informed salespeople calling at the most inopportune times. These operations rely on the slimmest of margins — if they make a sale on one call in a hundred, that's great.

Just like direct mail, this sieve approach isn't appropriate for the home-based guerrilla. Instead, you can turn the outbound telemarketing formula on its ear, using it as a highly focused, highly effective tool for generating new sales.

The guerrilla applies three rules to turn outbound telemarketing into a successful tool:

1. Be picky. Choose a small number of prospects. Do your research. Discover who they are and what they do. Find someone who knows

 TIP! Instead of using the phone for a direct sales campaign, try running a survey instead. Call ten hot prospects, ask them five or six questions, and promise to send them the results of the survey. Of course, your results will be accompanied by a detailed, personalized sales brochure!

them. Send the prospects a letter, a brochure, or a proposal.

2. Use your referral. If you can't mention a person, a colleague, or an organization, don't call.

3. Be slow and steady. If you try to make 110 calls a day, you'll be burned out for a month. Instead, try Richard Cassell's approach. Richard, who does voice-overs for radio, calls 10 people every day. In a month he can check in with the 200 people he's worked with in the past. These monthly reminders keep him at the top of his prospects' lists, ensuring that if there is work out there, he'll hear about it. As soon as he finishes the list, he starts again.

How to Get Your Call Through.

After picking your prospects, the biggest challenge is getting through. As we've become more wired, people have become defensive about the telephone. Voice mail, answering machines, and secretaries all stand guard. A few common-sense tips will make it easier for you to get through to the people you want to talk to.

First, be specific. Unless you can identify the name and phone number of each individual you need to talk with, you're not targeted enough. Guerrilla telemarketing is most effective with a list of ten, fifty, or even a hundred prospects. Much over that, and you're probably not being efficient. Calling names from a rented marketing list is not going to pay off. The best people to call, in fact, are already your customers.

Second, use your referrals. Most salespeople make cold calls. You can make "warm" calls by being sure you have a referral for every prospect. You'll have far better luck getting through if you're not calling as a stranger. "Hello, is John Jacobs in? Bill Weathers asked me to call him." A referral doesn't have to be a person, either. If you're the treasurer of the Chamber of Commerce or have just finished some work for Reebok, say so.

Third, warn the prospect in advance. If you send a prospect a distinctive, benefit-packed letter on Monday, it will be much easier to get him by phone on Friday. Even better, enclose a unique, business-related item with your letter. "Hi, is John Jacobs in? I'm calling about the stuffed owl I sent him on Monday."

TIP! Try to get the gatekeeper's name and use it often in your conversation. People love to hear their own names in conversation, and it may put the gatekeeper more at ease, breaking down any resistance to you.

Fourth, call at odd times. Eight in the morning and six at night are great times to find someone in. You can avoid interrupting meetings and the flow of the workday by calling when most others don't.

It's easy to focus all your attention on your prospect. But give a little to the gatekeeper. Take the time to get his name and ask him for advice on the best time to reach your prospect. Very often, the first step in a successful telephone sales call is to get through the receptionist, secretary, administrative assistant, or other person whose job is to screen the decision-maker from people like you.

What to Do Next.

Important! Once you get the prospect on the phone, be very clear about how long you want to speak and be sure that you're not interrupting.

> Here are twelve effective telephone techniques you should use when making a sales call:
> - Smile (it comes through in your voice).
> - Speak clearly and concisely.
> - Be enthusiastic.
> - Lower your voice pitch (for a more professional sound).
> - Speak slowly.
> - Welcome objections.
> - Talk directly into the mouthpiece.
> - Speak slowly (worth saying twice).
> - Speak in terms of benefits, not features.
> - Ask rather than tell.
> - Thank the listener for his time.
> - Follow up in writing.

Sometimes salespeople are so delighted to get through that they immediately launch into a pitch. Big mistake. Far better to take your time after receiving permission.

Hank Walshak makes a point of asking people "Is this a good time?" If the person says "no," he makes an appointment to call them back. He finds that people really appreciate such courtesy. The gesture makes a lasting impression, and people are likely to welcome his call the next time.

Once you begin the conversation, be clear about two things: the reason you're calling and the benefits you offer. It's unlikely you'll be able to sell anything to a stranger on the phone, so you ought to focus on setting up a meeting or sending a fancy brochure.

Hank Walshak says he never sells anything over the phone. His goal is to make appointments, to get his foot in the door. The questions he asks and the strategies he follows all lead up to that point.

The script is the sequence of questions and answers you think will lead to an appointment. Don't rely on your memory. Write out a script beforehand. Try to take into account all possible questions and objections and have an answer, follow-up question, and method of handling them all. Tape yourself delivering your script. Listen to yourself and practice.

Your questions should certainly include some that help qualify your prospect's decision-making powers. You should draw him or her out on personal matters. That will help establish a personal rapport. You should also ask questions that establish the level of need for your service and find out about special needs.

Your answers to questions posed by the prospect should always be "yes." Don't like that one? Try "can do." Or "no problem." You get the idea. Be positive when you talk to your prospect. Saying "no" and then trying to sell them on what you *can* deliver is unlikely to work.

Handling objections is the hardest part. Details on handling objections are in the next chapter, on closing the sale. But you won't go wrong if you rephrase objections, repeat them, and turn them into questions. "So you say you can't use cardboard packaging because it's too heavy. Then would lighter foamed plastic packages interest you?"

There's no such thing as an all-purpose script for telemarketing. Your product, your service, your competitive advantage, and your market all define exactly what you will say to your prospect.

Still, there are similarities among scripts. A typical telemarketing script might look like the following:

"Hello, Mr. Smith." (Say your prospect's name often.)

"This is John Doe." (Identify yourself clearly.)

"I'm calling for Doe's Copier Service." (Make it clear that this is a business call.)

"Jane Jones at ABC Business Systems suggested I call." (Always use a referral if you can.)

"Jane has been a long-time customer. How do you know her?" (A mutual acquaintance can be a springboard to establishing a personal tie.)

"I recently sent you a coupon for a free service call. Did you get it?" (Build on previous relationship-building efforts.)

"Mr. Smith, do you make arrangements for copier service at your company?" (Qualify your prospect. If not, get the name of

TIP! The telephone was invented for two reasons: talking and listening. The most important thing you can do when contacting a prospect by phone is to ask the right questions and then listen to the answers. Too many salespeople feel like they have to do all the talking.

the person you need. Use Mr. Smith as your referral.)

"Would you like to take us up on our no-strings-attached free service call, or should I send you more information?" (Ask questions that can't be answered by "yes" or "no.")

"Did you notice that we can service any major make of copier, and we offer one-day guaranteed turnaround on most repairs?" (Benefits, benefits, benefits.)

"Have you had to make any repairs or routine service on your copiers in the last year?" (If you do ask yes-or-no questions, make sure you know the correct answer in advance.)

"You have a regular service company? Have you been completely satisfied with the quality, cost, and turnaround time?" (Rephrase objections to defuse them and create an opportunity for yourself.)

"Do you know how many copiers you have, their remaining expected service life, and recommended maintenance schedules?" (Set up your next point.)

"Would you be interested in a *free* audit of all your copiers? I'll personally put together a detailed inventory of all your machines. Do you think that would be useful?" (Offer the prospect a reason to see you or talk to you again.)

"Would Wednesday afternoon be a convenient time for me to come in or is Thursday better?" (Go for an appointment, not necessarily a close.)

"Mr. Smith, I'll send you a letter detailing what we've talked about and give you a call Wednesday morning to confirm. I look forward to seeing you then. Good-bye." (Don't waste people's time. When you've got what you called for, let them go.)

Be sure to drop as many references and success stories as you can. Because you're not there in person, the visual clues and body language that establish your credibility are missing, so you need to pack your speech with as much reassurance as you can.

Here's one final example:

"Over the past year, I've created award-winning presentations for the New York Rangers, the owners of the Empire State Building, and McKinsey and Company. All my work comes with a money-back guar-

 TIP! Never lie to a gatekeeper. That's the best way to ruin both your credibility and your chance of getting through to your prospect.

antee, and I'm delighted to say I haven't had to give a refund in more than three years."

Keep talking like that and you're headed for success.

| **TIP!** | Most sales are made after the fifth call. Most salespeople give up after two. Don't give up! |

CLOSING THE SALE
SIGNING ON THE DOTTED LINE

PROFESSIONAL ORGANIZER SYLVIA JESSEY can't wait until a prospect says, "I like your service, but I don't have the money to pay for it. Thanks anyway." She knows that it's time to close the sale. How does she do it? Didn't she just get turned down? Nope. By offering to provide her services now and wait three months for her fee.

Why would Sylvia make such an unusual offer to someone who doesn't seem to want to do business with her? Because this home-based guerrilla recognizes that objections are really questions in disguise. Her prospects are actually asking, "Can I get better terms?" By answering "yes," she's able to close the sale. In exchange for the generous terms, she asks for three good referrals.

Marketing usually leads you to the moment before taking an order. This chapter is about the sale. Few products sell themselves. You have to ask for the sale. And for many home-based guerrillas, closing the sale is the hardest part of being on their own. Many would-be entrepreneurs have quit because the anxiety of closing the sale was more than they could bear. In fact, both the seller and the buyer are anxious about this moment.

As the seller, you're nervous because you might be rejected. The prospect is nervous about making the wrong decision. Studies have shown that a prospect's heartbeat actually increases up to 20% in the moments immediately preceding and following a "yes."

From the prospect's point of view, the two biggest issues are trust and fear. They want to trust you. They don't want to get ripped off, fired for buying the wrong thing, or stuck with a bad purchase. Ever heard the phrase "No one ever got fired for buying from IBM"? That truism helped the company sell billions and billions of dollars of products. Unfortunately, you're not IBM, so you'll have to work to build the trust you'll need.

SIX STEPS TO CLOSING SALES

Closing the sale is easier when you take the process one step at a time.

1. Qualify the Prospect.

You want to find people who really and truly need your product and are in a position to buy it. Customers are like needles in a haystack — if you sort through enough hay, you're bound to find them. Guerrilla marketing techniques like classified ads and direct mail are magnets that help you find the customer needles and get rid of the hay.

2. Contact the Prospect.

You only get one chance to make a first impression. Make it a good one. If you follow our advice about not skimping on the design, production, and writing of your printed materials and advertising, those parts of your marketing effort will work better. Follow the same advice when it comes to your personal contacts.

Does that mean always dressing up in a blue suit and red tie? Not at all. If you're a window-washer, you'd look ridiculous. A cleaning professional would look best in a sparkling uniform, maybe with a clean rag dangling from a hip pocket.

If you make contact by phone, try taping a few of your calls and review them with a friend later. If you make personal presentations, try practicing in front of a video camera and then watching it. Make sure you look and sound professional and that you are stressing the benefits of your service to the prospect. Look at yourself objectively and ask, "Would I buy anything from this person?"

3. Ask Questions.

Discover exactly what your prospect needs. People aren't always truthful — they may be trying to spare your feelings, or they may have an agenda that isn't clear. Maybe the clothing buyer is looking for a line of

One way to hone your closing skills is by asking your present customers why they bought from you. You may be surprised by their answers, but you'll learn a lot about the way prospects perceive you and your product.

clothes that will get her mentioned in *Vogue* as opposed to a line that will just make money. You won't know unless you ask.

4. Ask for Objections.

Remember Sylvia the organizer? Objections are a salesperson's best friend. Take your time. Have the prospect outline the exact problems with your offer. Don't be in a hurry to answer the objections. Try to get all of them out in the open.

5. Ask the Obligating Question.

This is the critical moment, and the one that most neophytes are afraid to try. "Mr. Prospect, if I can show you that our product easily overcomes [objections 1, 2, and 3], are you prepared to order today?" If the answer is "no," do some detective work to find out why. If the answer is "yes," respond to those objections and ask for the sale.

6. Get the Order.

Get it in writing. And do it today. Bring an order form or standard contract and fill it out as you talk. There are ways to help the prospect act now without being pushy.

None of these six steps can stand on its own. They must be coordinated and orchestrated, always leading to your ultimate objective. The first two steps — qualifying and contacting prospects — are covered throughout this book. Here we will cover the next four.

ASKING QUESTIONS

It's easy to overlook this part of the sales process. You're very close to your business. You think about it all the time. You're confident that you already know what the customer wants. And you're probably wrong.

In every business, there are hundreds of conflicting agendas. Purchasing agents have many reasons to buy products. Sometimes it's to satisfy a real need, and sometimes it's just to keep the company budget looking good. A newspaper editor is pressured to hire his brother-in-law but hates his writing style. It goes on and on.

The only way to find out what people really need and want is to ask and then listen. If possible, you want to do this in person. Later on, we'll describe how to close the sale when you sell by mail or catalog. Here are some effective questions:

- "How did you get into this business?" A standard icebreaker, it works because most people love to talk about themselves. It will give you tips about the person's background that will help you build a relationship and tailor your proposal.

- "How did you find us?" This one is great for any business that gets unsolicited calls. The answers may even alert you to hidden weaknesses or unexploited strengths in your advertising.

- "What's the best product of this type you've ever used? What did you like about it?" Sure, you're asking for a prospect to reminisce about something you can't control — a competitor, perhaps. But the answer will also clue you in to the client's standards and values. Meet those standards with your product, and you have a sale. And the next salesperson to ask this question will be hearing about you!

- "What's the worst experience you've had with this type of product?" You may hold your breath while awaiting the answer for fear that your product may come up. Relax. Remember, objections are questions. If you answer them properly, usually the sale is yours.

- "What did you like about it?" Use this question any time your prospect expresses enthusiasm — about anything. It keeps the exchange positive and gives you more insight into what motivates the prospect to sign on the dotted line.

- "What was it that bothered you?" Pull this one out when your prospect complains about a past experience. First, though, agree: "I can understand that" or "I know what you mean." Otherwise, you may sound as though you're disagreeing or even arguing — an often fatal error.

- "What's more important — speedy delivery or low price?" The answer to this one may surprise you. Many people consider themselves frugal but actually will pay handsomely for what they want and need. Highlighting various aspects of your product or service (don't limit it to delivery; cover payment terms, service, and the like) will help you craft your own offer.

- "Who has to approve this purchase?" People may be touchy about this one. You don't want to offend an important gatekeeper by slighting

 Selling is nothing but a transference of feeling. If you don't believe that your product is the solution to the prospect's problem, it's time to move on.

his or her authority. You can't afford to spend all your time talking with non-decision-makers, either. And if they *do* make the buys, you're at least in the right place.

- "When can this purchase be made?" Even a person with buying authority has to have funds. Budget schedules, purchase order turn-around time, and plain old business needs make timing all-important in closing a sale. It may be best to leave literature and wait to close for another day or, even better, close the sale but save delivery and payment for the next month, quarter, or whatever.

- "Why?" The all-purpose, all-important question. Understanding motivation is the key to a successful closing. You may not phrase it quite so baldly every time you use it. (You don't want to sound like a two-year-old.) But this question, in one form or another, underlies all others.

You can go overboard with questions. You can spend too much time thinking about your next question and not listening to the answers. That's like panning for gold and tossing out the nuggets without looking in the pan. Listen carefully for two things:

Content is the first thing you'll hear. The factual information your prospect is giving you is important. Home in on key phrases, especially those that are repeated. Jot them down. Be obvious about writing down hard facts. Clients are impressed that you're paying attention.

The emotional tone of an answer may not seem as important as the factual message. But it is even more important for building a relationship. Try to pick up on your prospect's feelings. Is he wary? Does she seem confident? Voice inflections and nonverbal cues can give you explicit information about a prospect's state of mind. This kind of information is even more valuable than factual content because the prospect is often unaware it's there.

Naturally, you'll also be asked questions. You may feel threatened and attempt to answer them all with a fully detailed, comprehensive presentation. But hold on! Printed marketing materials must answer questions before they are asked, but that's not as important when you're closing the sale in person.

When a prospect asks a question, resist opening the floodgates. Some

TIP! Realize that you won't close every sale and know when to give up. If you have visited with a potential client twenty-five times and still can't close, recognize that your time will probably be better spent pursuing hotter prospects.

salespeople talk too much, answering questions at great length or not waiting for questions at all. That's natural. We're excited about our business. We want to share the good news.

But giving too much detail can paint you into a corner. If the client asks about March delivery, answer only that question. Don't add, "Whew! I'm glad you didn't ask about August. We're booked that month and couldn't get a shipment out to save our lives." The client's next question may have been, "What about late summer?"

Whenever you're asked a complicated or loaded question, it's a good idea to repeat it in your own words. That shows the prospect that you're listening and also prevents you from answering a question that wasn't even asked.

Talk slowly. Give the prospect a chance to interrupt. Then take a break to listen. Ask another question of your own. Over answering may make you look too eager or as if you're trying to snow the client. Understating her needs will keep things relaxed, comfortable, and more conducive to a sale.

ASK FOR OBJECTIONS

Objections are better than questions. They uncover the prospect's *real* concerns. Rather than brushing off objections, successful guerrillas encourage them.

Not that objections aren't scary. You probably can think of at least a couple that you'll be hard-pressed to answer. Why would you want to ask for something you can't deal with? Here are two compelling reasons:

First, when a customer expresses an objection, it's also an expression of interest. Think about it. If somebody tried to sell you something for which you had no conceivable use, would you tell them the price was too high and the delivery terms were lousy? Naturally not. You'd just laugh, ignore them, or flatly refuse. You'd only raise specific objections if you really wanted the product but had reservations.

You have to have interest from the prospect to make a sale. When you hear an objection, you should perk up, not poop out. It's a positive sign.

Second, some objections are real stumpers. If you haven't qualified a

 TIP! Don't rush the sales cycle. Don't even attempt to close the sale until you have built a solid relationship with your prospect and are convinced that what you have to sell is what she needs. If you don't believe it, neither will she.

prospect well, you may even find yourself agreeing with unanswerable objections to your product — a Pulitzer Prize–winning author won't get paid his going rate by the PTA newsletter. All the negotiations in the world aren't going to close that sale.

If qualified prospects repeatedly have valid objections that keep you from closing the sale, it's time to reconfigure, reprice, or reposition your product or service.

Manageable objections usually fall into one of three broad categories:

1. The Request for Information.

Almost any prospect asks for information. Of course, any guerrilla salesperson is perfectly prepared to give it — unless the request isn't recognized because it comes in the form of an objection. Here are requests for information that seem like objections:

> Dawn Orford has found that being a home-based business owner can sometimes get in the way of closing the sale. She has found a way to turn what seems to many to be a disadvantage into a great advantage. When a prospect asks her "do you work out of your home?" Dawn anticipates the real issue and addresses it head on with this answer: "Yes, our offices are, in fact, located in my house. However, I think what you're asking is 'what level of commitment, quality, and service will I receive.' Whether we work from a house or a downtown office building, I guarantee in writing that you will get the absolute highest level of service from us." With a couple of sentences, Dawn refutes one more objection to closing the sale.

- I've got to have it before you can deliver it. (The prospect is asking: Are better delivery terms available?)

- I can't use this color. (The prospect wants to know: Are other colors available?)

- Cash is too tight. (The prospect wants to know: Do you offer financing or other payment terms?)

Try to rephrase any objections you hear into questions like this. Even better, jot down common objections and translate them into questions before you make your sales call. Like a United Nations translator, you'll automatically and instantly understand them as questions, not roadblocks. And you'll find they pose few problems to a close.

2. The Stall.

Sometimes when a prospect is not quite ready to buy, he or she will say something like:

- I need to sleep on it.

- I need to check with my spouse (or boss or partner).

- I can't do a thing until payday.

This can be a puzzling objection, especially if it comes just as you thought a solid prospect was about to commit. Often, it means there is another objection the prospect hasn't mentioned. What to do? Confront it directly. Say, "If today was the day after payday, what would keep you from signing the contract?" You'll either find out the real objection or get a commitment.

3. The Farfetched Objection.

A customer suddenly brings up an issue from so far out in left field that you aren't sure you heard correctly. You probably did. Irrational, half baked objections surface fairly often. Here are a few common examples of farfetched objections:

- "The corner of this box is bent. Are you trying to sell me damaged goods?"

- "It's not just your prices that are too high — it's the whole industry!"

- "I always swore I'd never buy anything on Saturday. And I just realized today is Saturday."

Who can blame you for wondering what's going on? Actually, it's fairly simple. Farfetched objections surface when customers feel they have lost control. They may feel pressured or confused. This unanswerable objection is like a wild grab for the steering wheel.

What to do? Don't bother countering the objection — it will lead you in a futile direction. Let them have control back and they may settle down.

Sometimes the best response to a bizarre objection is to give the prospect exactly what he wants. Take the pressure off. Insist that he's not ready to buy. In fact, say you're not sure if this is the product for him.

This jujitsu approach puts the onus back on the prospect. You've essentially asked him to convince you that he should buy. And you've given him control.

Fish for Objections.

You should seek out at least one objection. Ask your prospects what they want. Then fish for an objection by telling them you can't do that.

 TIP! Talk about your past successes when trying to close the sale. Remind the prospect that you have dealt with similar clients before. That will reduce the risk and make it easier for the prospect to say "yes."

Sound crazy? Here's why it isn't:

First, as we've already seen, an objection means your prospect is interested. You're being taken seriously.

Second, letting your prospects express a negative opinion gives them a sense of control. It's an important step on the road to building a relationship.

Finally, an objection is an opportunity to close. Your prospect is implying that if you answer this objection, he will buy. Sure, there may be other objections. But an objection successfully countered is a major step on the road to closing.

You can greatly increase your chances of successfully asking for and overcoming objections of all kinds if you master a few simple techniques for dealing with them. It's not hard.

First, write down each objection as you hear it. Don't be shy about it. Let the prospect see you taking notes. This demonstrates that you're listening carefully. It also helps you see patterns. Record only the main points. Trying to write down every detail may distract you from the sales dialogue you're having. And if you sense your taking notes is making the prospect uncomfortable, ask permission. It's another way to show you care.

Then restate an objection in your own words to make sure you *both* understand it. This is an incredibly powerful and absolutely critical step to overcoming objections.

How many times have you had a frustrating or pointless discussion with someone and realized later that you were talking about the same thing in different ways? Or maybe you were given a brilliant answer to the wrong question. You can avoid this misunderstanding by rephrasing and repeating objections back to the prospect.

If a client says, "I've got to get you to cut your $100 price by 20%," restate it by saying, "If I understand you, you're saying $80 is what you can pay, right?" Now, listen carefully to what is said next.

You may still have it wrong! The client may say, "You don't understand. Price is unimportant. I just have to be able to show my boss I got a 20% discount." Now you're getting somewhere.

Rephrasing and restating objections is a chance to gain understanding — and to show it. It's a superb way to leverage your personal relationship-building skills.

Always use a talking pad to discuss the objections. You're taking notes to help your memory and your analysis. You're repeating and rephrasing the prospect's questions to clarify matters. Combine these two potent tools with a talking pad.

Here's an example of how you might use a talking pad to help sell a high-quality widget to a customer who cares about price. Your conversation is in quotation marks, what you write on the pad is in roman (all caps).

"You mentioned that the price of the widget you're buying is important. If I may, let me point out that there's a huge difference between PRICE and COST. The engineers at Roco and Avic, two of our biggest customers, have shown us that they prefer the cost of our widget. Let me show you":

US

PRICE: $200
YEARS OF SERVICE GUARANTEED: 10
COST PER YEAR: $20

THEM

PRICE: $150
YEARS OF SERVICE GUARANTEED: 3
COST PER YEAR: $50

"I hope you'll agree that while their widget has a lower PRICE, our widget has a lower COST. And that's what you really want, isn't it?"

Notice that when you're finished, the prospect is left holding a piece of paper that hammers home your message. You can use a talking pad to deal with multiple objections, too. List them; then deal with them one at a time in black and white.

ASK THE OBLIGATING QUESTION

While you'll be tempted to answer each objection as it's brought up, don't. Instead, collect a few, then try to answer them in a batch. But before you do, you need to ask the obligating question.

This question is your way of flushing out any remaining objections

 Send a thank-you note (along with your written guarantee) to every new client.

and then setting the stage for asking for the order. Remember, you're not asking for the order yet. Instead, you're just asking for permission to ask for the order later.

"If I can show you that [we answer objections 1, 2, and 3, as listed on this pad], are you prepared to buy this product today?"

Doesn't sound like much. But it's the last stop before decision city. In a moment or two, you'll know whether your attempt to close was a success or failure. It's normal and natural to veer away from a chance of rejection.

We've already said that few products sell themselves. If you are to sell and succeed, you must ask people to buy, explicitly. But sometimes that knowledge isn't enough.

Think up several obligating questions and go over them in your mind. Write them down. Now say them out loud. Repetition will help them spring to your lips more readily. It will also remove some of their intimidating importance.

Imagine the most awful, nasty rejection you can. Now imagine a prospect laying it on you when you ask for the sale. Next, ask yourself two questions:

Could you handle it? Of course you won't like it. But are you willing to pay the price of rejection? If not, someone else ought to make the sales calls.

How will you respond? Think of a response you'd be comfortable with. Blaming the prospect is a bad idea. It builds resentment. Instead, try to understand that if your closing ratio is 20%, that means you've got to be rejected four times before you make a sale with the fifth person. The prospect who rejects you is helping you get one person closer to that fifth prospect.

NINE TOOLS TO CLOSE THE SALE

Every close is different because every customer is different. Some people can't be sold. Others don't have to be.

What a guerrilla needs is a set of basic closing tools. They can be evaluated before or (after you've practiced enough) while you're in the middle of a challenging sale situation. One of them may be able to turn a near miss into a close.

 TIP! You can't trick someone into buying from you — not if you want to build solid relationships. Instead, focus on benefits. If you can discover what your prospect needs, you can close the sale.

1. Offer a Free Gift with an Order.

This can change the focus in the consumer's mind. How else do banks lure $10,000 certificates of deposit with the promise of a toaster that sells for $10 wholesale? The customer is thinking, "I want that toaster." So the bank gets the deposit, probably at a lower interest rate than it would have had to offer otherwise.

If you can come up with a gift that sounds expensive but isn't, great. Better, offer a gift that is not widely available anywhere else. It might be a book or pamphlet you wrote. It might be a free fitness session. The gift doesn't have to be related to your product or service. It has to relate to the desires of your prospects.

2. Offer a Limited-Time Offer.

This provides subtle pressure to decide *today*. As a general rule, a sale delayed is a sale denied.

Caution: never tell a customer an offer is for a limited time unless it is. Truth is a basic rule of selling. However, there's nothing wrong with structuring or restructuring an offer so that it truly is for a limited time.

3. Stress Your Testimonials.

There's no reason why you should do all the talking. Let your current satisfied customers talk for you. Never underestimate their power to close for you. If everyone else is doing it, it seems safer.

4. Focus on Word of Mouth.

Prospects who come to you are far easier to close.

This is another reason "How did you hear about us?" is such a terrific question. If you know a prospect heard about you from a friend or relative, you know you have a much better chance of eventually making a sale. If you don't know it, you may give up too early. Don't let these hot prospects go undetected.

5. Offer a Guarantee…and Mean it!

A solid guarantee removes risk in the prospect's eyes. If you eliminate risk, you make closing easier.

Be sure to make your guarantee meaningful. Make the terms realistic, and make it simple for the buyer to collect if the guarantee is trig-

 The selling process doesn't end when you close the sale. In fact, that's the start. Repeat business is far more profitable, and word of mouth won't happen without customer satisfaction.

gered. And make sure the prospect hears about it during your sales pitch.

6. Don't Push Too Hard.

Sales is not a game of power or manipulation. Never argue with a prospect. Once you start an argument, you lose.

Let's say you're selling home computers. A prospect says he has three already and adds, "So you're wasting your time with us." It may seem as if you have two options: argue or hang up. Do neither. Agree, then ask if the ex-prospect (who clearly knows the value of what you're selling) knows of three people who could use a PC. It won't get you an immediate sale, but it may lead to one.

7. Don't Be Afraid to Agree with an Objection.

Sometimes you have to say "You know, maybe you're right. Maybe you don't need this product." Or "You can't afford it." Or "I don't think you'd get the best out of it."

8. Don't Ask for a Yes.

Use an alternate-choice close. Instead of saying "Will you buy this?", try "Do you want it in black or will red be all right?" or "Should we deliver it, or do you want to pick it up?"

The basic idea of the alternate-choice close is to avoid giving the prospect a choice between something and nothing. Instead, offer your prospect a choice between accepting your offer in one way or accepting it in another way.

9. Don't Wait Too Long.

If you believe in your product, you won't hesitate to sell it. You should ask for the order often. Aim to ask for the order at least three times in a typical presentation.

Zig Ziglar tells of the young salesman who was asked, "Are you trying to sell me something?" Defensively, he answered, "No, no...Of course not." The obvious response? "Well, then why are you here?" Of course you're trying to sell something — something that will benefit the person you're talking with. Make that clear from the start and you can have a productive, professional interaction.

 Don't be falsely convinced that you have closed a sale just because the prospect agrees that your product is good, will fill her needs, and is affordable. You haven't closed the sale until she agrees to act! Don't stop selling until she "signs on the dotted line."

10. Don't Fail to Close on Selling Yourself.

You now have the weapons and the insights to market your home-based business with confidence and aplomb. Is there a major barrier you should know about? There sure is: You may run short on patience. But you've got enough going for you to give you an infinite supply of patience:

- You are running a home-based business, riding the crest of a wave, and being provided with support services never before available. The odds are in your favor.

- You realize that successful home-based businesses don't get that way in a hurry. Figure on a minimum of a year to be an overnight success, with three years being a more realistic expectation.

- You have an understanding of what marketing really is and how it really works, enabling you to market more effectively to more genuine prospects, while spending less money in the process.

- You are, or you better be, a person with a two-way brain. People with one-way brains read books but do not act upon what they learn. People with two-way brains learn, then translate their wisdom into action.

- You are a guerrilla, endowed with the common sense to realize that successful marketing plans, marriages, and home-based business are the result of commitment. You've made that commitment. You can't miss.

We wish you good luck and good fortune on your quest to climb the ladder of evolution from someone else's office to your own home.